The Marshall Cavendish

International

WILDLIFE

ENCYCLOPEDIA

VOLUME 13
LEA – MAN

MARSHALL CAVENDISH
NEW YORK · LONDON · TORONTO · SYDNEY

Revised Edition Published 1991

Published by Marshall Cavendish Corporation
2415 Jerusalem Avenue
North Bellmore, NY 11710
USA

Printed and bound in Italy by LEGO Spa Vicenza

Library of Congress Cataloging-in-Publication Data

Marshall Cavendish International wildlife encyclopedia/general
    editors, Maurice Burton and Robert Burton.
        p. cm.
        ''Portions of this work have also been published as The
    International wildlife encyclopedia, Encyclopedia of animal life and
    Funk & Wagnalls wildlife encyclopedia.''
        Includes index.
        Contents: v. 13. LEA-MAN.
        ISBN 0-86307-734-X (set).
        ISBN 0-86307-806-0 (v. 13).
        1. Zoology–Collected works. I. Burton, Maurice, 1898-
    II. Burton, Robert, 1941-   . III. Title: International wildlife
    encyclopedia.
    QL3.M35 1988
    591'.03'21–dc 19

Volume 13

Leathery turtle

The leathery or leatherback turtle or luth is the largest sea turtle, and also differs from the others in the structure of its shell. The upper shell or carapace is made up of hundreds of irregular bony plates covered with a leathery skin instead of the characteristic plates of other turtles. There are seven ridges, which may be notched, running down the back, and five on the lower shell, or plastron.
Leathery turtles are dark brown or black with spots of yellow or white on the throat and flippers of young specimens. They grow to a maximum of 9 ft, the shell being up to 6 ft, and may weigh up to 1 800 lb. The foreflippers are very large; leathery turtles 7 ft long may have flippers spanning 9 ft.

Rare wanderer

The leathery turtle is the rarest sea turtle and lives in tropical waters, probably spending more time in deeper water than other turtles. Little is known about its habits and even its breeding haunts are not well known. Leathery turtles are known to breed in the West Indies, Florida, the northeastern coasts of South America, Senegal, Natal, Madagascar, Sri Lanka and Malaya. The breeding populations are small and predation of eggs by men and dogs endangers the populations of some beaches. Although generally restricted to warm waters, leathery turtles are occasionally found swimming in cooler waters or washed up on beaches, especially when carried by adverse winds or currents. They have been seen off Newfoundland and Norway in the north, occasionally straggling as far south as New Zealand.

Unlike some other turtles leathery turtles do not carry encrustations of barnacles and seaweeds. This may be due to the very oily skin. Although the leathery turtle is described here as the rarest of the turtles, it is of interest to note that it has been increasingly reported in recent years, especially in the North Atlantic. One reason for this, possibly the main reason, is that fishermen have switched to faster, motorized vessels.

A soft diet

The stomach contents of leathery turtles show that they feed on jellyfish, salps, pteropods (planktonic sea snails) and other soft bodied, slow-moving animals, including the amphipods and other animals that live in the bodies of jellyfish and salps. Leathery turtles have been seen congregating in shoals of jellyfish and the 2–3in. horny spines in the mouth and throat are probably a great help in holding slippery food.

Early morning and the leathery turtle completes her task of egg-laying by filling in the nest hole. This rare sea turtle spends more time in deep water than any other turtle, coming onto land only to nest and lay eggs. Each female comes ashore, usually late at night, about four times a season.

Leathery turtle *(Dermochelys coriacea)*

Breeding in bands

Female leathery turtles come ashore in small bands to lay their eggs, usually late at night. They come straight up the shore to dry sand, stop, then start to dig the nest. They do not select the nest site, by digging exploratory pits and testing the sand, as in green turtles. A hollow is excavated with all four flippers working rhythmically until the turtle is hidden. She then digs the egg pit, scooping out sand with her hindflippers until she has dug as deep as she can reach. About 60–100 eggs, $2-2\frac{1}{4}$ in. diameter, are laid, then she fills the nest with sand and packs it down. Finally she masks the position of the nest by ploughing about and scattering sand, then makes her way back to the sea. Each female comes ashore to lay about four times in one season. The eggs hatch in 7 weeks and the babies emerge together and rush down the shore to the water.

The Soay beast

In September 1959 a large animal was seen in the sea off Soay, a small island off the Isle of Skye, western Scotland. There was much speculation at the time about what it could be. The two men who saw it gave a description of it and each made a rough sketch of it. The interest was increased by the fact that on at least one occasion many years previously a similar animal had been reported from these same waters. So the Soay Beast, as it came to be called, passed into history as an unsolved mystery, possibly a sea monster, probably one of the several different kinds of sea-serpent reported at various times. All these things seemed possible when one looked at an artist's impression published at the time. In due course Professor LD Brongersma had little difficulty in showing that, beyond reasonable doubt, the animal was nothing more than a large leathery turtle. In this he confirmed the opinion of Dr JH Fraser of Aberdeen, expressed in May 1960, a few months after the sighting was reported.

If the artist's impression was misleading we cannot blame him. He had only the verbal statements to go upon, together with two crude sketches. The real moral is that one should pay more attention to Occam's Razor. William of Occam (now Ockham) was a 14th century English scholar and philosopher who expounded the principle that if there are two or more theories to account for something, choose the simplest.

class	**Reptilia**
order	**Testudines**
family	**Dermochelidae**
genus & species	***Dermochelys coriacea***

◁△ *What brings tears to a turtle's eyes? The answer might be to remove sand from its eyes on the rare occasions when the leathery turtle comes ashore to nest and lay eggs. The accepted theory is that by crying the turtle gets rid of the excess salt that has been swallowed with gulps of sea water. Whatever the reason, the turtle looks very sad.*

◁ *The leathery turtle ranges into cooler waters than the green turtle—see the map on page 1096.*

Lechwe

Lechwe are antelopes closely related to both waterbuck and kob, and there are two species. They have a longish, rough coat but no mane, and the long, slender, lyre-shaped horns, in males only, are curved twice. They have no face-glands and the glands of the groin are rudimentary. The smaller, known as Mrs Gray's lechwe, lives in the swamps of the White Nile and the Bahr-el-Ghazal. It is 35—40 in. high; the adult male is a reddish black-brown with a white pattern on the head, extending from in front of the eyes to behind the base of the horns, then down the back of the neck to a white patch on the withers. The chin and upper lip, the middle of the belly and the inner surfaces of the hindlegs are white, and there is a broad white band above the hoofs. The female and young are yellow-brown, with weakly-defined white areas on the head, and no white on neck or shoulders. 'Mrs Gray' is a rare species and little is known about it.

The common lechwe of the Zambesi region is 40 in. high with long, coarse hair and very differently coloured. The three well-marked subspecies are so different they need to be described separately.

The most widespread is the red lechwe, of the upper Zambesi and its tributaries, western Zambia, southeastern Angola, the Ngami swamps of Botswana and the Caprivi Strip of Southwest Africa. It is light reddish-tawny with the whole underside, from belly to chin, white; the fronts of the forelegs and of the hind-shanks are white. The second subspecies is the Kafue Flats lechwe, found only on the marshes of the middle Kafue River, a tributary of the Zambesi. In this the long spreading horns reach 32 in., and the black line up the foreleg expands on the shoulder to form a conspicuous patch. In the third subspecies, the black lechwe, the black has spread still farther, so it covers the whole of the head, upper parts and fronts of the limbs. The black lechwe is found from Lake Bangweulu to Lake Mweru and over the border of Zambia into Zaire. It is smaller than the other two. A male of the red or of the Kafue Flats subspecies weighs 220—260 lb, and a female 165—185 lb, but male black lechwe weigh only 150—200 lb.

Graceful antelopes—herd of red lechwe peacefully grazing in Lochinvar Estate Reserve. Never very far from water these animals are considered to be semi-aquatic, often spending all day submerged up to their necks in water.

Sustained by floods

On the vast marshes known as the Kafue Flats, 140 miles long, 10—30 miles wide, covering 2 500 square miles of the Zambesi basin, lives the best-known of the lechwes. Here, the rains come from November to March, and the flats become flooded; from April to October they are dry, with water virtually confined to the river itself. The lechwe is therefore semi-aquatic, living on the margins of the river and in the shallows, feeding on grasses both in the water and on land. The herds are very loose and flexible, and the sexes tend to keep in separate herds. When the floods are at their height, at the end of the rainy season, the lechwe are confined to a narrow belt extending ¾ mile inland from the water's edge. At this time there is not much grazing to be had in the water, and they feed mainly on dry pastures which have long been ripe and so have little food value. The lechwe are generally in poor condition. In June and July the floods recede, revealing hundreds of square miles of grazing, and their condition improves dramatically. Later in the year when the rains begin again the storms drive the other animals, such as zebra and gnu, off the flats and the lechwe have the area to themselves.

Survival of the very fittest

Fierce ruts take place from late October until early January, but it goes on sporadically until the end of the rains. Mock fights between the bucks occur at all seasons, but at this time fighting is in deadly earnest, and wounding, laming, and broken horns are common. Among black lechwe the fights are sometimes fatal. The bucks make staccato grunts which are audible a quarter of a mile away. No territories are formed; the males merely gather harems around themselves. Of the one-year-old does, 40% breed, and nearly all breed in subsequent years. Gestation lasts 7—8 months. The lambs are dropped from May to December with a peak from mid-July to late August. The does leave their herd singly or in groups and give birth in patches of tall grass, often on high ground surrounded by floodwater. The lambs stay hidden for 3—4 weeks before rejoining the herds with their mothers. Half of the lambs die before weaning (which occurs at 3—4 months) then in the dry season many lambs of the yearlings die of a warble infestation. Thus, selection in the lechwe is very severe indeed and those that survive are, in strictest Darwinian terms, 'the fittest'.

Males are full-sized at 4 years, females at three. The males' horns appear first at 5—6 months; at a year they are 6 in. long; at 2 years, 15 in.; at 3 years, 23 in.; at 4 they average 32 in. (the record is 36¼ in.). The black leg-stripe appears at 3—4 years of age.

Hyaena foes

Lechwe are preyed upon by hyaena, crocodile, cheetah and wild dog, in that order of severity. Lions prey on them in areas where there are any. Python and leopard probably prey on the young; also eagles, and perhaps shoebills. Many infants are drowned during stampedes.

Slaughter in the marsh

Lechwe are of immense importance in the ecology of the marshes. They provide vast quantities of dung, which makes the area fertile and able to support large numbers of animals, not only lechwe, but also gnu, zebra and domestic cattle. Their dung also improves the fertility of the water, which makes for a prosperous fishery and abundant waterfowl. The amount of protein on the hoof, on the wing and in the water on the Kafue Flats is very great. In the 1930s it was estimated there were 250 000 lechwe on the Flats, probably an over-estimate with

Okapia

Molly Zaloumis

CT Duval

the true figure nearer 160 000. In 1960 there were only 25 000. What caused this precipitous drop? The answer probably lies in the *chila,* a large annual hunt lasting 2−4 days, traditional with the Ila tribe. Groups of lechwe would be encircled, trapped with their backs to deep water, and killed. The largest *chila* in modern times was in 1956, when over 1 100 men took part. Young boys came along to herd the cattle which dragged the 175 meat carts. Over 2 000 lechwe were killed in 2½ days, 63% being females. In previous *chilas,* the proportion of females may have been even higher. They are easier to kill because they tend to concentrate in the shallow flooded areas, which are more suitable for *chilas,* the male herds favouring dry land. Also their skins are softer and more pliable, and were much favoured as cloaks to be worn at puberty and funeral rites.

Chilas were stopped in 1957, but the results are still to be seen. About 60% of the adult population are males; elsewhere in Zambia only 20−30% are males. Now that *chilas* no longer take place, and that the Zambian government has purchased Lochinvar Ranch (101 077 acres on the south bank of the Kafue River, where many of the lechwe live) with a view to creating a Lechwe

National Park along the Flats, the future of this race seems assured.

The black lechwe have also been overhunted. The population has been steadily reduced from a million in 1900 to 150 000 in 1934, to 16 000 in 1959, and seems not to have dropped below this since then. The Zambia Wildlife Society has been active in pressing for the creation of a Black Lechwe Reserve to preserve this race. Fortunately in this case the sex ratio seems to have remained steady at 33% males. In Mrs Gray's lechwe, which may have a somewhat different type of social organisation, the sex ratio is almost exactly 50:50.

◁ *The chase is on—red lechwe stampede. Until about twelve years ago there used to be an annual hunt,* **chila,** *held by the Ila tribe when hundreds of lechwe would be killed. As a result the population was considerably reduced. Fortunately they are now legally protected.*
△△ *Shaggy but rare species—Mrs Gray's lechwe. The distinctive white neck patch makes it easy to distinguish from the other lechwes.*
△ *Shy youngster—Kafue Flats lechwe.*

class	Mammalia
order	Artiodactyla
family	Bovidae
genus & species	***Kobus leche leche*** red lechwe **K. leche kafuensis** Kafue Flats lechwe **K. leche smithemani** black lechwe **K. megaceros** Mrs Gray's lechwe

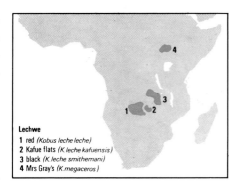

Lechwe
1 red (*Kobus leche leche*)
2 Kafue flats (*K. leche kafuensis*)
3 black (*K. leche smithemani*)
4 Mrs Gray's (*K. megaceros*)

1427

Leech

*Leeches are most closely related to earth-worms. An obvious difference, however, is the sucker at each end of the body, the hind one being more powerful than the one around the mouth. The body is segmented as in earthworms but each segment is divided into several smaller rings. Leeches have no bristles like those used by earthworms in moving, the only exception being a small fish parasite of Lake Baikal **Acanthobdella** which is intermediate in other ways too.*

The medicinal leech, once plentiful but now restricted in its distribution, is about 5 in. long when extended, less than half this when contracted. Its colour pattern varies, but usually it has a pair of longitudinal red stripes on a greenish background on its upper surface, with black markings towards the sides. Some of its patterns were copied on women's clothing in the early 19th century. There are five pairs of simple eyes near the front end and additional pairs of light-sensitive areas at intervals along the body.

The horse leech varies from dark grey-green to a paler yellow-green. Among smaller species are some that are markedly flattened and prettily patterned. Some marine leeches parasitic on fish have a row of gills down each side.

Infection the real danger

Leeches are mainly animals of fresh water. They swim by vertical undulations of the body, or loop about by attaching each sucker alternately. Of the species parasitic on fish, however, many are marine and there are also various unpleasant land leeches that attack man (and other animals in damp places) notably in southeast Asia. These may lurk on vegetation as well as on the ground and readily penetrate clothing, creeping perhaps through the lace-holes of boots, then bloating themselves with blood before being detected. As the three sharp jaws make their Y-shaped incision, saliva is injected that may contain, as well as an anaesthetic, a substance to prevent the blood clotting and another that causes the blood vessels to dilate so improving the flow of blood. Some leeches may take as much as ten times their own weight of blood before dropping off and can, not surprisingly, survive many months without feeding again. The medicinal leech takes only 2–5 times its own weight. The danger from leeches is not the loss of a little blood: it is the infection of the wounds that may follow. Another danger is that leeches may enter the mouth or nostrils and, too swollen to escape, block the breathing passages. They may also cause internal bleeding in these places. Such dangers, which can be fatal, are the result of incautious drinking from some of the springs and wells, especially in the Near East, and many cattle, horses and dogs are killed in this way in India. In detecting their prey, leeches may respond to shadows, to disturbance of the

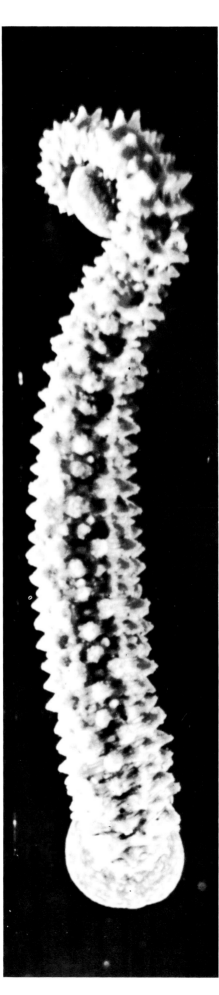

GS Giacomelli

water, to chemicals released into the water by the prey and to the heat of the body.

The medicinal leech, a native of Asia as well as of Europe, and introduced into North America, feeds on the blood of large mammals and also of frogs and even small fish. The horse leech, on the other hand, deserves neither its common name nor its scientific name of *Haemopis sanguisuga* for it is not a blood-sucker. Instead, spending much time out of water, it feeds on slugs, earthworms, insects or decaying flesh, as do some of the other smaller leeches. The leeches of the family Erpebdellidae swallow worms and other small animals whole or suck the juices of snails or insect larvae by means of a proboscis—they can even suck the whole snail out of its shell.

Leeches make good mothers

Leeches are hermaphrodite, but cross-fertilisation is the general rule. Sperms may be introduced directly into the body of another, much as in mammals, sometimes after a simple courtship display, or may be deposited in a sticky packet, or spermatophore, on the body of the partner. In the latter case, the sperms somehow pass through the body wall to get to the ovary. The fertilised eggs are usually laid in a cocoon secreted by the clitellum, as in earthworms (p. 815). In some leeches the parent broods the cocoon and ventilates it with undulations of the body. In such species the embryo later becomes attached to the underside of the parent, while still in the egg, by a sort of ball-and-socket joint. Then, after hatching, the young ones remain on the parent for weeks or months. One species, *Marsupiobdella,* which feeds on African freshwater crabs, has a brood pouch opening on its underside.

External use only

In these days of antibiotics and transplants, when the average European has never seen a leech, it is surprising to learn that the use of medicinal leeches was once so great that in 1824, for instance, 5 million were imported into England or that, in 1833, over 41 million were imported into France. For centuries a great variety of ills was treated by the letting of blood by this and other means: delirium, madness, skin diseases, tumours, whooping cough, gout, obesity, teething troubles, and many more, varying with the opinions of the doctor. Headaches might be treated by a ring of a dozen leeches on each temple, or colic by as many as fifty applied to the abdomen. Small wonder that physicians became known as leeches! Though the routine application of these animals behind the ears of children to draw blood away from the sinuses of the brain may seem nonsensical now, it is said that leeches can be helpful in relieving the congestion around a black eye—but even this is doubtful.

Though leeching has been practised in Asia from time immemorial, it was during the 2nd century BC that Nicander of Colophon first recorded the therapeutic use of the leech and both Pliny and Galen discussed the matter. Snipping off the hind end of the leech was recommended to improve the flow of blood. Galen referred to various methods of removing leeches accidentally swallowed, such as draughts of urine, vinegar or snow, but Avicenna (979–1037) recommended the avoidance of such emergencies by drawing a thread through the tail so should the patient accidentally swallow the leech it could be pulled out.

Leeches were usually collected by agitating the water and netting them as they floated up, but another method was simply to wade barefoot. As Wordsworth put it in *Resolution and Independence*, '. . . stirring thus about his feet the waters of the pools where they abide'. At one time, the leech trade was centred in France, but early in the 19th century, the supplies dwindled in France, then in Portugal, Spain, Bohemia and Italy. Prices rose as the marshes of Hungary, too, began to fail towards the middle of the century, leaving Poland, Russia, Turkey and Syria as the main sources of the supply of leeches. The use of leeches also started to decline, however, in the latter half of the century and has now virtually ceased in Europe.

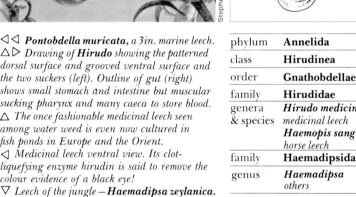

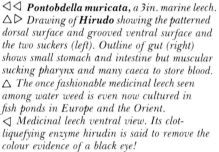

◁◁ **Pontobdella muricata,** *a 3in. marine leech.*
△▷ *Drawing of* **Hirudo** *showing the patterned dorsal surface and grooved ventral surface and the two suckers (left). Outline of gut (right) shows small stomach and intestine but muscular sucking pharynx and many caeca to store blood.*
△ *The once fashionable medicinal leech seen among water weed is even now cultured in fish ponds in Europe and the Orient.*
◁ *Medicinal leech ventral view. Its clot-liquefying enzyme hirudin is said to remove the colour evidence of a black eye!*
▽ *Leech of the jungle —* **Haemadipsa zeylanica.**

phylum	**Annelida**
class	**Hirudinea**
order	**Gnathobdellae**
family	**Hirudidae**
genera & species	*Hirudo medicinalis* medicinal leech *Haemopis sanguisuga* horse leech
family	**Haemadipsidae**
genus	*Haemadipsa* others

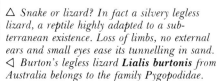

John H Tashjian at San Diego Zoo

Graham Pizzey: Photo Res

△ Snake or lizard? In fact a silvery legless lizard, a reptile highly adapted to a subterranean existence. Loss of limbs, no external ears and small eyes ease its tunnelling in sand.
◁ Burton's legless lizard **Lialis burtonis** from Australia belongs to the family Pygopodidae.

Legless lizard

There are only two species of legless lizard in a family related to the slowworm, and both live in a restricted habitat in California. They are more specialized for burrowing than even the slowworm. Up to 10 in. long, the legless lizards have no limbs, the body is covered with smooth scales and the lower jaw is countersunk to improve the soil-moving efficiency of the head. The eye is very small with moveable eyelids to protect it, and there is no external ear. This not only means one less obstacle to a smooth passage through soil but an animal living so completely underground has no need to pick up soundwaves; vibrations through the soil are enough to guide it.

One species, living in a coastal strip, 600 miles long by 150 miles wide, from San Francisco southwards, is divided into two subspecies. The better known of the two is called worm lizard or silvery footless lizard. This lives up to 3 000 ft above sea-level. It is silvery grey, 7½ in. long, with a dark line down the centre of the back and one along each side. The other, the black legless lizard, blind worm or blind snake, about the same size, is black, and it is found only in the neighbourhood of Pacific Grove, whereas the other is found along the coast from Contra Costa County to Baja California. A second species lives along the coast of Lower California and on the adjacent island of Geronimo, after which it is named.

Burrows to avoid heat

Legless lizards spend much of their time burrowing. They feed on insects and other arthropods in the soil, such as woodlice and mites, centipedes and millipedes, which they find by smell and touch. The depth at which the lizards are found varies with the time of year. In winter and spring they are 6–12 in. down when the soil is not heated to any great depth. As summer progresses they go deeper, to 3 ft in early summer and to 4–5 ft in midsummer. Several American zoologists have looked into this. They have taken the temperature of the lizard immediately on capturing it, the temperature of the soil at the depth of the lizard's burrow, and also the air temperature. There is a fairly steady correlation between these, with the lizard's body temperature about 1°C above that of the soil and the temperature of the soil about 2°C above that of the air. So we know that the lizards follow a 'temperature gradient', moving down as the soil heats up in summer and up as the soil cools in winter (in subtropical California).

Under logs and boulders the temperatures will be more constant and legless lizards are sometimes found there. They will come to the surface at night and there are at least two records of legless lizards crawling across streets, in Bakersfield, Kern County, moving from a piece of uncultivated ground. One had travelled 500 yards when it was picked up.

Young are born alive

As with many other legless lizards, the Californian species bear live young, the eggs hatching just before or at the moment of leaving the female's' body. The baby lizards are 2½ in. long of which nearly a third is tail. They reach maturity at the age of 3 years, at a length of 8–10 in.

Short legs, big waggle

It is interesting to compare the American legless lizards with the legless lizards of the family Pygopodidae found in Australia. One of them, found over much of that continent and known as Burton's legless lizard, *Lialis burtoni*, is 30 in. long, of which 20 in. is tail and only 10 in. head and body. This, to start with, is in striking contrast with the proportions of a snake, in which the tail is usually about an eighth of the total length. Burton's legless lizard has two tiny flaps—all that is left of its limbs—near the vent. It feeds on other lizards known as skinks, does not burrow but worms its way through grass, and is sometimes locally called a grass snake. This is excusable since, like the Californian legless lizards, it moves like a snake.

Long-bodied lizards with short legs walk at times with considerable sideways movements of the body. That is, they waggle their bodies. As the legs grow shorter and the body, including the tail, grows longer and more slender, the reptiles crawl rather than walk. With the total loss of the legs the way of moving over the ground becomes serpentine. This is an advantage, as in the Australian legless lizards, for moving through grass. It has its limitations for one living underground, as in the Californian legless lizards, because it restricts them to soft soil or loose sand.

class	**Reptilia**
order	**Squamata**
suborder	**Sauria**
family	**Anniellidae**
genus & species	***Anniella pulchra pulchra*** *silvery legless lizard* ***A. pulchra nigra*** *black legless lizard* ***A. geronimensis*** *Geronimo legless lizard*

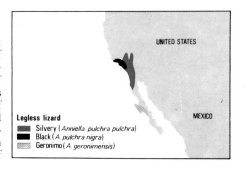

Legless lizard
■ Silvery (*Anniella pulchra pulchra*)
■ Black (*A. pulchra nigra*)
▨ Geronimo (*A. geronimensis*)

UNITED STATES

MEXICO

Lemming

This is a rodent linked in our minds with mass suicides and one of the main aims here must be to put this longstanding story into perspective. The mass migration story is usually told about the Norwegian lemming, which is only one of 12 species of these rodents, living in the northern hemisphere. These include five species of collared lemmings in Arctic Canada, Siberia and European Russia, two bog lemmings of North America, one wood lemming from Norway to Siberia and four species of true lemmings of northern Europe, Asia and America. All are stout bodied 4–6 in. long with 1 in. or less of tail, with thick fur, blunt muzzles, small eyes, and ears small and hidden in the fur. Here we concentrate on the Norwegian lemming, which also ranges across Sweden, Finland, and northwest Russia.

Safe under snow

The Norwegian lemming lives at 2 500–3 300 ft above sea level, above the line of willows. In summer lemmings occupy moist stony ground partly covered by sedges, willow shrubs and dwarf birch. They make paths through the carpet of lichens and rest in natural hollows or cavities in the vegetation. In autumn they move into drier areas, at or about the same level as the summer quarters. In winter they usually live under the snow, protected from cold and from enemies, building rounded nests of grass that are sometimes left hanging on twigs when the snow has melted. They make extensive tunnels under the snow. Because their food is lichens, mosses and grasses wintry conditions do not interrupt their feeding and in an ordinary winter they continue to breed.

Several litters in a year

Several litters are produced by each female in a year. The gestation period is 20–22 days and each litter has 3–9 young, born in a spherical nest of shredded fibres, moss and lichens, made under cover of a rock or in a burrow.

The lemmings' enemies are stoats, weasels, rough-legged buzzards, ravens, longtailed skuas, the various members of the crow family and snowy owls. In winter the lemmings are safe under their covering of snow from all but stoats and weasels, and even they are present in fewer numbers. So there is a marked difference in predation between summer and winter.

Mass migrations

Lemmings, like many small rodents, are subject to fluctuations in numbers from year to year. They also share with voles, to which they are closely related, cyclic rises and falls in numbers. The populations build up over a period of years to abnormal numbers and then comes a crash fall and numbers are reduced to normal. The interest, so far as lemmings are concerned, lies in the causes of these rises and falls and in what actually happens when their numbers are

△ *Norwegian lemming—the biggest and best known of all lemmings with its characteristic markings. It is thought to be the only existing mammal indigenous to Scandinavia.*
▽ *In peak years the Norwegian lemming is completely unafraid of predators including man.*

abnormally high. The scientific explanation in the past has been that in years of abnormal numbers the lemmings migrate down the mountainsides into the fertile valleys in search of food. This is near the truth. The popular stories, aided by artists' impressions in the form of pictures, based on local hearsay, is of columns of lemmings in headlong dash down to the sea, where they are drowned in a sort of mass suicide.

In the last 20 years this has been particularly studied and several informed accounts have been published, including one by Kai Curry-Lindahl, in *Natural History* for August–September 1963.

A matter of climate

Curry-Lindahl gives three main reasons for the population explosions. First, an early spring and a late autumn produce favourable climatic conditions that not only yield an abundance of food but give the lemmings a longer period in which to take advantage of it. Secondly, mild winters with thaws and also severe winters are damaging to winter breeding. In winters that are between these extremes there is a high rate of breeding and of survival among the young. The third is that because of the lack of enemies during winter there is no brake on the mounting increases in numbers resulting from the first two.

Panic among the masses

In the years 1960-61 there was an explosive eruption of lemmings, in three waves, one in May, the second in June and a third in August. They were noticeable mainly in places where there were obstacles to their spreading out evenly, for example, a long lake or where two rivers meet making a kind of funnel. Then there comes an accumulation of lemmings followed by a kind of panic in which they march recklessly but not in any special direction. They may go up the mountains as well as down into valleys. They may go to any point of the compass. They may go over glaciers or swim across rivers or lakes or, as in Norway where the mountains run down to the sea, into the sea. Lemmings swim well, with the body and head well out of water. Their fur is waterproof, so they take no harm from a wetting, and if the water is calm they can cross a river or lake. If it is choppy, as in the sea, or on lakes in windy weather, many are drowned.

During 1960 there were abundant lemmings but no crash in numbers. This came in 1961, and the explanation is probably supplied by an investigation of the collared lemming in America by WB Quay. Briefly, he found that under warm conditions especially when there was stress or tension the lemmings suffered an upset of their internal balance. One symptom was abnormal deposits in the blood vessels of the brain. The result was severe exhaustion and finally death.

Lemming *(tribe Lemmini true Lemmings)*

No massed columns

Another study of Norwegian lemmings has shown that although the animals live solitary lives on the mountain tops, and are probably intolerant of each other's company, when they move down into the valleys they become gregarious. For a while, therefore, they crowd together, feed amicably side by side and share burrows. This may be what happened in 1960. As their numbers rise, so the stress mounts, with a high death rate, as in 1961. The important thing to remember is that there are no massed columns of lemmings all flowing in one direction until they reach the sea.

Rains of lemmings

The first published account of the suicidal tendencies of the Norwegian lemmings was written by Zeigler, a geographer of Strasbourg, in 1532. It was based on information given him in Rome by two bishops from Norway. He told how in stormy weather lemmings fell from the sky, that their bite was poisonous and that they died in thousands when the spring grass began to sprout. In 1718, Joran Norberg, writing of the march of Charles XII's army over the mountains in Norway, said 'People maintain that clouds passing over the mountains leave behind them a vermin called mountain mice or lemmings'. Eskimos in Arctic America have similar beliefs about rains of lemmings, and their name for one species in Alaska – anticipating by many years modern ideas about UFOs – is the 'creature from space'.

Walter Marsden

class	**Mammalia**
order	**Rodentia**
family	**Cricetidae**
genera & species	**Lemmus lemmus** *Norwegian lemming* **Dicrostonyx hudsonius** *collared lemming, others*

▽ *Lemmings usually migrate in search of food over the Norway mountains at a fixed altitude, as shown by arrows. But when there is a population explosion panic follows and the lemmings move haphazardly in all directions. They do not rush to water to commit suicide, in fact they swim quite well, but many die of stress leading to exhaustion.*

Walter Marsden

Walter Marsden

△ *Alaskan varying lemming or collared lemming in its white winter coat. It is the only true rodent that becomes white in winter, being brown or grey in the summer. Like all lemmings it is small and fat and has a short tail. Its small ears are completely covered by thick fluffy hair. It can burrow under snow and wander over it even in the dead of the Arctic winter.*

◁ *These footprints in the Norwegian snow beside the ski tracks show that the lemming does not hop but walks.*

▽◁ *Snow claws of the Alaskan varying lemming. In winter the third and fourth claws of the forefeet become enlarged by the growth of a thick horny shield under the permanent claws. The purpose of this shield is not known but probably has something to do with its snow-shovelling activities.*

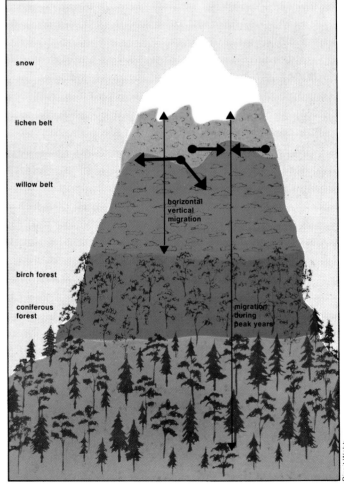

snow

lichen belt

willow belt

horizontal vertical migration

birch forest

coniferous forest

migration during peak years

Birgit Webb

Lemur

Lemurs are primates related to monkeys, and they vary in size from that of a small dog to that of a mouse. They are confined to Madagascar, and the more specialised indri, sifaka and aye-aye are treated in separate articles. The remainder belong to a single family, Lemuridae, although it has been pointed out by the French zoologist Jean-Jacques Petter that there are three very distinct groups. To the first group belong the mouse-lemurs and dwarf lemurs: small, rarely over a foot long, with long, somewhat bushy tails, short pointed faces, their coats red to grey with a white or yellow underside. One species, the fork-crowned lemur, has a pattern of black stripes on its head joining the dorsal stripe to the rings round its eyes.

The second group are the 'true' lemurs, 20–40 in. long, also with very long, bushy tails. The black lemur has tufted ears and fringed cheeks. The males and young are black with bright yellow eyes, and the females pale reddish-yellow. The ring-tailed lemur, grey with a black-and-white ringed tail, has a white face with black muzzle and black eye-rings. The ruffed lemur, the largest, is panda-like, black and white or sometimes red, black and white. The gentle lemur is brown with white eye-rings and short snout.

The sportive or weasel lemur stands alone, to form the third group. It is about the size of the largest of the dwarf lemurs, with large eyes and ears and a short face. It leaps from one upright stem to another with its long hind legs, like an indri.

Many lemurs are found almost everywhere on Madagascar, mostly in the forest but also in the drier scrublands. The ring-tailed lemur lives, however, in the southwest of the island, the ruffed lemur in the northeast. The rarest and most localised species are the hairy-eared dwarf lemur, of which only a few specimens are known, thought to be from the eastern forests, and the broad-nosed gentle lemur, equally rare and localised in just a few places in the east.

Petticoat government

The larger lemurs are mostly crepuscular, that is, they come out at twilight, although they come out by day when the sky is overcast. Ring-tailed lemurs are more diurnal, however, while ruffed lemurs are nocturnal. All lemurs like to sun themselves, sitting upright with their arms spread to the sides as if praying. The larger lemurs, especially the black and ring-tailed lemurs, live in social groups of a dozen or so, often with more males than females. The males have a rather strongly marked rank order—but all females are dominant to any male! The animals make grunts to keep the group together, and the ring-tailed lemur makes miaow-like sounds. The ruffed lemur utters a series of intense roars, increasing in volume, followed by loud clucks.

The ring-tailed and gentle lemurs have scent glands on the shoulders and forearms, the latter being provided with spurs, used in marking territories by touching branches with them. The shoulder glands are found in males only. They draw their tails across the glands and then flick them, dispersing the scent into the air. The black lemur rubs its forearms on branches although it has no glands there, while most other species of lemurs mark with urine or faeces. It is believed these methods of marking are connected with the social ranking of the males.

The mouse- and dwarf lemurs, and also the sportive lemur, are nocturnal, sleeping most of the day in nests made among foliage or in holes in trees. The two dwarf lemurs are remarkable in having a less efficient temperature regulation than most mammals. The larger of them has short phases of torpor lasting 2–3 days, while in the smaller species the torpor may last a week or more, the animal getting very fat beforehand and its temperature, while torpid, falling near to that of the surrounding air. In eastern Madagascar it probably spends most of the dry season in this condition, which is known as aestivation.

Mainly vegetarian

The sportive lemur is entirely vegetarian, feeding on leaves, fruit, bark and buds. The dwarf and mouse-lemurs eat fruit, berries or insects, but probably not leaves or bark. The larger lemurs eat more leaves and fruit, but no insects.

Different kinds of infancy

Lemurs are sexually inactive for most of the year. Mouse-lemurs come into season every 35 days or so between September and January. Larger species are in season from April to June; sportive lemurs from May to July; normally each cycle lasts only a month. Mouse-lemurs have a gestation of 2 months, and have 2–3 young; other lemurs have a gestation of 4½ months, and have only a single young. The dwarf and mouse-lemurs bear their young naked and undeveloped, and the mother puts them into a nest made in the foliage. The young ruffed lemur is also born at an early stage of development and the mother builds it a nest in the fork of a tree, which she lines with fur from her sides. In other lemurs the young are born fully furred and able to move around. The young black lemur clings to its mother's belly; so does the young ring-tail for a few days, after which it is carried on its mother's back. The young sportive lemur is well-developed and moves around on its own near its mother. The mother, when leaping to another tree, carries it in her mouth.

The mouse-lemur has the fastest development of any primate. It is independent of its mother after four months, and fully mature at 7–8 months. Even so, this is a longer period of maternal care than in any non-primate mammal of a size comparable with this small lemur. Maternal care is a well developed feature of mammals but is most obvious in the primates, the group to which humans belong.

Air raids

Compared with other places, Madagascar is almost idyllically free of predators. The small civets, such as the fossa, might sometimes eat small or young lemurs but the main danger is from the air. Eagles glide silently through the treetops and will round a corner and snatch up a small lemur at a moment's notice. Eagles and men are 'mobbed' by ring-tailed or black lemurs with a series of increasing grunts, working up to a crescendo, all in unison, repeated every 2–5 seconds. To escape, the black lemur can jump as much as 27 ft; dwarf lemurs scuttle away into the foliage; sportive lemurs leap from trunk to trunk.

Nosey lemurs

By calling lemurs 'lower' primates we imply that, although related to monkeys, apes and man—the 'higher' primates—their ancestors became separate from our own before a high intelligence, binocular vision and skilled use of the hands had been developed. In fact, of course, lemurs *are* primates, and have achieved a certain advancement over other mammals in all three of these fields. In higher primates, the increase in the sense of sight has been linked with a loss in the sense of smell while lemurs have retained a better sense of smell. Indeed, the ring-tail has, in the words of CS Evans and RW Goy, after their recent study, a 'complex olfactory repertoire'. But calling them 'lower' does not mean that they are in all ways primitive and unspecialised. In certain respects lemurs have undergone striking specialisations all their own. They have, for example, a unique and as yet unexplained structure of the ear region of the skull. They have nails on all digits except the 'index' toe, which has a sharp claw used for grooming. Their lower incisors and canine teeth are procumbent and flattened like the teeth of a comb—and this, it seems, is exactly what they are used for—for combing their fur—and a long, horny filament, the sublingua, underneath the tongue is used to scrape the accumulated dirt out of the 'comb'.

class	Mammalia
order	Primates
family	Lemuridae
genera & species	*Allocebus trichotis* hairy-eared dwarf lemur
	Cheirogaleus major dwarf lemur
	C. medius fat-tailed lemur
	Hapalemur griseus gentle lemur
	H. simus broad-nosed gentle lemur
	Lemur catta ring-tailed lemur
	Lepilemur mustelinus sportive lemur
	Microcebus murinus mouse-lemur
	Phaner furcifer fork-crowned lemur
	Varecia variegata ruffed lemur

Lemurs in the trees

Ring-tail parade (right). With tails held high a group of ring-tailed lemurs stroll off to the undergrowth leaving a forgotten member of the band sitting on the ground.

With the greatest of ease and without a trapeze a ring-tailed lemur flies through the air (below left).

An inquisitive dwarf lemur (below right) and a wide-eyed mouse-lemur (bottom right). They are small lemurs, rarely more than a foot long, and have small pointed faces with large appealing eyes. Both nocturnal, they scamper, squirrel-like, about the trees using their long bushy tails as balancers. These small lemurs are able to store quantities of fat in the ends of their tails, and also in the rump in the case of the mouse-lemur, to use up during the hot dry seasons when food is scarce.

RD Martin

Startled look. A rare photograph of **Avahi laniger**, probably the first one to be taken in the wild, with the mother carrying her baby on her back (right). The avahis belong to the family Indridae and are close relatives of the lemurs, but are specialised leaf-eaters with powerful cheek teeth for chewing and reduced front teeth.
Fixed stare from a gentle lemur (below left). This is one of the larger species of lemur. Among this tangled mass there is a lemur nest! (below right). Not all lemurs build nests; young ring-tails are carried on the mother's back like the avahi above. But in the mouse-dwarf and ruffed lemurs the young are born at an early stage of development so the mother puts them in a nest made in the fork of a tree or in foliage.

RD Martin

RD Martin

Leopard

The size of the leopard, one of the big cats, varies from one part of its range to another, the range being southern Asia and much of Africa. The males may be up to 8 ft long, including 3 ft of tail, and weigh up to 150 lb. The females are smaller. The colour and length of the fur also vary with the locality and with the climate. Its ground colour is a tawny yellow, whitish on the underparts, with many small black spots which on most of the body are arranged in rosettes. 'Panther' is an alternative name for 'leopard' often used to distinguish black individuals.

C Guggisberg: Photo Res

A Kerneis: Jacana

W Myers: WWF

Powerful cat

Always shy and wary, with keen senses, the leopard's ability to hide makes it harder to track down than a lion or tiger. Leopards will live wherever cover is available: in forest, bush, scrub or on rocky hillsides. They are mainly solitary except at the breeding season. When living in areas where they are hunted they are nocturnal. Elsewhere they are active in the early morning and again in the late afternoon then continuing into the night. During the day, where they are nocturnal, or in the heat of the day, leopards lie up in 'day-beds' in thick undergrowth. Leopards are very powerful for their size and can carry a large kill up into

◁ *Too late: the prey's first inkling of danger was this leopard's charge, leaving time for only a futile bound before death.*
▽ *Treetop larder: hunger brings a leopard back to a carcase stored for future reference.*

KH Stanley

a tree. They climb trees well and often take a kill up into a fork to cache it. They are powerful leapers and one which leapt over a railway truck 7 ft high had made a leap 20 ft long. The leopard's voice is a grunting or harsh coughing, or a sawing roar.

Strong food preferences

A leopard will eat almost anything that moves, from dung beetles to antelopes larger than itself. The full range of prey includes impala, steenbuck, bushbuck, reedbuck, nyala, klipspringer, waterbuck, zebra foals, wildebeest calves, warthog, dassies, as well as cane rats, hares and ground birds. The smaller prey are taken more especially by the young and the old. A favourite trick of leopards in their prime is to lie along a branch waiting for prey to pass beneath, then to drop onto it, seizing it by the throat or, at times, sinking the teeth into its skull.

It has several times been found that individual leopards have a taste for one kind of prey. One fed largely on impala, another ate only bushpig and would travel 2 miles each night from its day-bed to hunt, never molesting the game around its day-bed. The famous leopard of Kariba seemed to eat nothing but the fish *Tilapia*, lying at the water's edge until the fish came to the surface, then catching them with its paw. Another leopard is said to have caught frogs. This tendency to specialise may explain the man-killers. Once they have killed a human they develop a taste for the flesh. It may be the same with leopards that kill livestock because there are known cases of leopards living near farms that never molested the cattle. Some leopards seem to be unusually partial to dogs as food. There are records of leopards eating leopard. It seems that when males fight, over territory or in the breeding season, one may be killed and the other eats it.

Cubs are born blind

There are no firm records for the times of breeding but it seems likely that it may take place at all times of the year. Gestation is 90–105 days and the number of cubs at a birth is usually 3 but may be 1–6, born blind. The cubs stay with the parents until sub-adult.

Leopards in pest control

Because of the attacks of individual leopards on human beings, domestic stock and dogs, they have been mercilessly hunted in parts of their range. It is now realized that leopards can confer a direct benefit where they prey on antelopes, bushpigs and baboons that ravage crops. One leopard is known to have lived almost entirely on cane rats that are a scourge of several crops, such as grass and sugar cane.

Even more intensive hunting for the sake of their skins has further reduced their numbers as compared with former times. At a meeting of the Survival Service Commission of the International Union for the Conservation of Nature at Nairobi in 1963 it was reported that nearly 50 000 leopard skins were being poached in East Africa each year, as a result of women's fashions. Most of these were smuggled out through Somalia and Ethiopia because elsewhere leopards were protected by law. A full-sized leopard coat takes 5–7 skins. The poachers, who received £1 per skin, were catching the animals by nooses, springjaw traps, poison and other agonising methods. The numbers are now down to 20 000 a year, or less.

Come and get it

Mr S Downey, honorary game ranger for the former Tanganyika Territory, reported in 1953 seeing a leopard with the carcase of a Thomson's gazelle in the lower branches of a tree. A lioness trotted over, looked at the kill and leapt into the tree. The leopard, without hesitation, took the carcase to the topmost branches of the tree, moving the carcase this way and that, getting it nicely balanced in a fork. The lioness seemed to decide she was at a disadvantage. She jumped down from the tree, trotted over to a shady spot 50 yards away, lay down and went to sleep. The leopard seemed now to believe it safe to remove its kill. It descended with it to the ground and made for a larger tree nearby. Suddenly the lioness was on her feet and the leopard raced back to the first tree and up into the branches, only just ahead of the lioness, but sufficient to take the gazelle out of the lioness's reach to the top of the tree once more. Altogether, it is a first-class illustration of the strength and agility of the leopard.

B Lomstrand: Jacana

class	**Mammalia**
order	**Carnivora**
family	**Felidae**
genus & species	***Panthera pardus***

Leopard seal

The leopard seal has perhaps the most notorious reputation of any seal, but as will be seen this is quite unjustified. It is usually solitary and is found all around the Antarctic, usually at the edges of the pack ice. It is the only seal in which the adult females are always larger than the males. The males grow to a maximum length of about 10 ft and a weight of 600 lb, while the females may grow as long as 12 ft and a maximum weight of 1 000 lb. The two sexes are much alike in appearance. They are grey, darker on the back and paler on the underside, with a variable number of darker grey spots, especially on the throat and flanks. Leopard seals have often been described as reptilian. The body is long, thin and flexible and at first sight the head seems a few sizes too large. The mouth, which can be opened very wide, adds to the ferocious appearance. It has large teeth, those in the cheeks having three distinct cusps.

Leopard seals live in the outer edges of the Antarctic pack ice but the sub-Antarctic islands of South Georgia, Heard and Kerguelen are usually well populated by leopard seals especially in the winter months. They are occasionally found in the southern parts of South America and South Africa, and not infrequently in southern Australia and New Zealand. The farthest north that a leopard seal has been recorded is Rarotonga in the Cook Islands, just 20 degrees south of the equator in the Pacific. The number of leopard seals has been estimated by observations from polar vessels in the pack ice to be around 250 000 animals.

Sleeping ashore

Leopard seals usually live out to sea among the ice floes and are rarely seen on the shores except when they prey on penguins. When they do come ashore it is usually at night, and they come onto land or onto ice floes to sleep after feeding. Rarely are more than three or four seen together at one time. They move over land or ice with the fore-flippers pressed to the side of the body and clear of the ground, and heave themselves forward rather like a caterpillar, looping forward on the chest and rear end, alternately doubling up and stretching out.

Lurking for penguins

The food of the leopard seal includes fish, squid and krill as well as penguin. The leopard seal has a distensible trachea, which collapses to allow large chunks of food to be swallowed. One leopard seal, for instance, was found with a penguin in its stomach which it had swallowed whole. Around islands such as South Georgia and the South

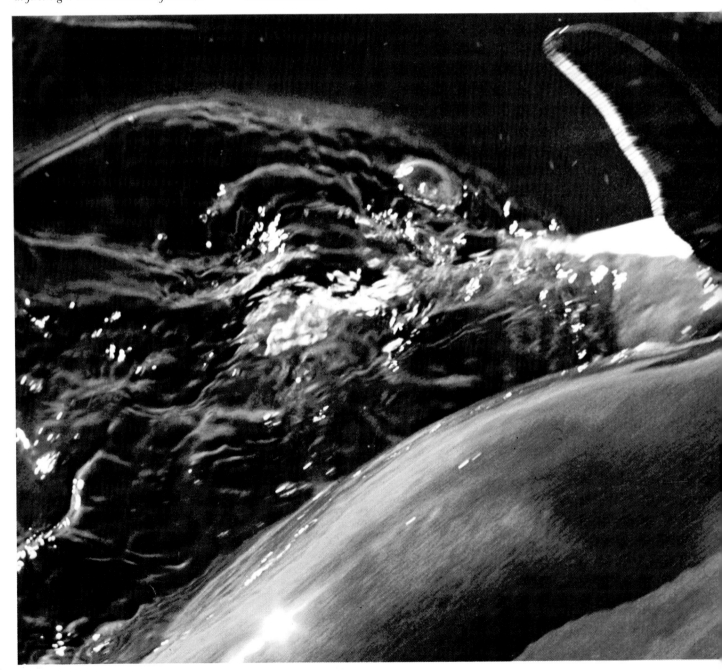

Sandwich Islands where there are very large penguin rookeries there are also substantial numbers of leopard seals. Inevitably they feed on penguins as they are a readily available source of food. The seals lie in wait just offshore from the penguin rookery and attack them as they set out for the feeding grounds or as they come ashore from feeding at sea. The leopard seals chase the penguins and grab them from underneath and then shake them violently to tear off pieces of flesh.

It was once thought that penguins were the main food of leopard seals, but it is now realised that only a few leopard seals have the habit of lying in wait near penguin rookeries. The reason for the mistaken view is probably that men in the Antarctic most often saw leopard seals near penguin rookeries and did not realise that many more were fishing out to sea.

A penguin can outmanoeuvre a leopard seal and many escape to the shore, narrowly avoiding the seal's teeth, but if the seal can head a penguin off it can wear it down by continually chasing it around. Only very rarely have leopard seals been seen chasing penguins on land or ice. Usually the penguins are quite safe on land and will walk unconcernedly past a sleeping leopard seal.

Icy nursery

Leopard seals breed on the pack ice. The pups are born between November and January; at birth they are about 5 ft long and probably weigh about 60 lb. Lactation lasts about 2 months, then the parents mate again and separate until the following year.

Curious, not ferocious

The leopard seal has a reputation for ferocity in the Antarctic and has even been described as a maneater. There is not much cause for this, and in the few instances when men have been attacked it is usually the men who first provoked the seal. Such cases, together with many stories of men being chased, have helped bolster the idea of the ferocious seal. Leopard seals follow small boats, leaping out of the water and even climbing aboard. They come on land to investigate men and swim around aqualung divers. This is most likely curiosity on the part of the leopard seal, but one cannot blame the men involved if they are unwilling to put this to the test. The sight of the large head and rows of teeth, together with the memories of leopard seal stories, make discretion the better part of valour.

class	**Mammalia**
order	**Pinnipedia**
family	**Phocidae**
genus & species	*Hydrurga leptonyx*

Careless, slow or just unlucky: an Adélie penguin in a leopard seal's jaws. Penguins can usually outmanoeuvre this bulky enemy.

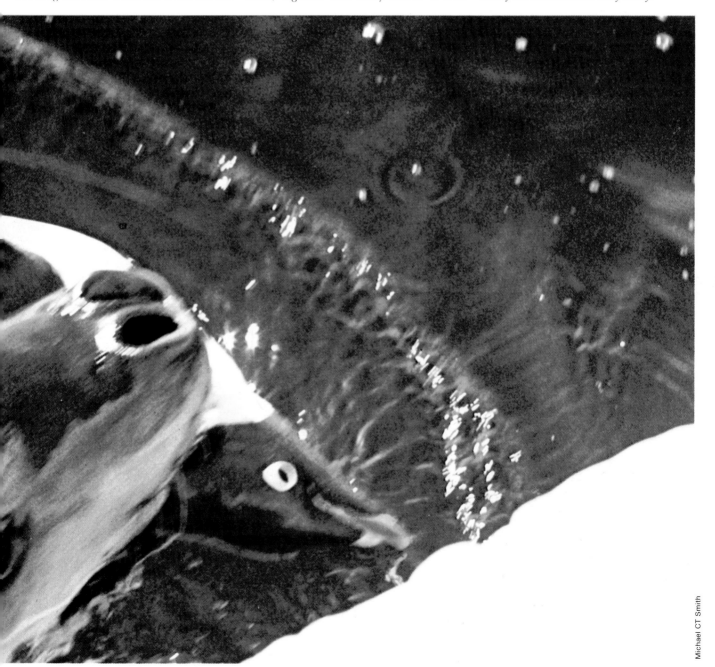

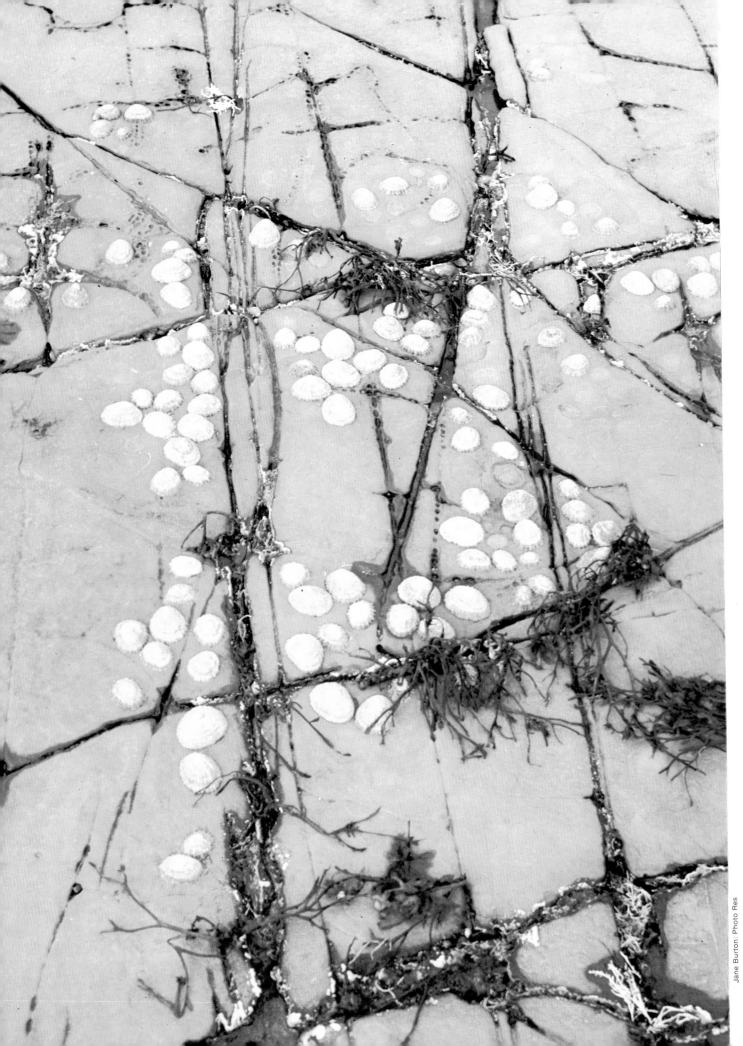

Limpet

'Limpet' is a term applied to various kinds of snails which, while not necessarily closely related, have two features in common. They cling tightly to rocks or other surfaces and they have a shell that is more or less tent-shaped. The best-known is the common limpet, flither or papshell, and related to it is the pretty little blue-rayed limpet or peacock's feathers, found on some of the large brown seaweeds at low tide, and the tortoiseshell limpet **Acmaea tessulata.** The keyhole limpet **Fissurella costaria** is named for the hole in the top of its conical shell and the slit limpet **Emarginula elongata** for the slit at the front. The Chinaman's hat **Calyptraea chinensis,** which retains a trace of its spire, is classified in the separate order Mesogastropoda. The limpet form has also been evolved independently in certain relatives of the pond snails. This repeated emergence of the limpet form in the evolution of snails is due to the advantage it gives in withstanding the action of fast-moving or turbulent water. It is particularly advantageous on rocky, wave-battered shores and it is on these that the common limpet, the main subject of this article, is so successful and abundant.

Under the protection of its ribbed, conical shell, which may reach nearly 3 in. in length, the common limpet has a grey-green oval foot with a large flat adhesive surface. At the front is the head with its big ear-like tentacles, each bearing an eye near its base. Lining the shell around its margin is the thin layer of tissue that secretes it and all around this skirt and lying in the space between it and the foot are many small ciliated gills and short tentacles.

Limpets are not suckers

The common limpet may occur in great numbers on rocky shores, from low water even to above the highest tide levels, provided the rocks are well splashed and shaded. As well as being resistant to wide temperature fluctuations limpets may flourish where the sea is greatly diluted with fresh water. Shells high up on the shore tend to be taller and thicker, especially near the apex, than those living lower down or in rock pools. Limpets are very difficult to dislodge, unless taken by surprise, and Reaumur found that a weight of 28 lb could be supported when attached to the shell.

Carving itself a niche

As well as giving resistance to wave action the ability to cling serves to protect limpets from predators. They are, however, a favourite food of oystercatchers and rats may take them in large numbers, dislodging them by a sudden movement of the jaws. It has been known for the tables to be

△ **Patella** crawling over glass showing the muscular foot and head and marginal tentacles.
◁ Village of common limpets.

△ Flattened delicate tortoiseshell limpet.
▽ The unmistakable blue-rayed limpet with its rows of vivid blue spots.

▽ Chain of slipper limpets (with shore crabs). Bottom ones are females, the upper younger ones male and those between of intermediate sex.

turned and for a rat to become trapped with its lip under the shell, and birds have been caught by their toes. That man at one time ate them in large numbers is evident from the shells in his old kitchen middens.

A further advantage is that the limpet can seal a little water amongst its gills and so avoid drying up when the tide is out and in this, as well as in its clinging, it is helped by the close fit of shell to rock. This comes about in the first place from the choice of a suitable resting place, but it is improved both by the growth of the shell to fit the rock and by the abrasion of the rock to fit the shell. Each limpet has a definite 'home' to which it returns after each feeding excursion. Often the rock becomes so worn the limpet comes to lie in a shallow scar of just the right size and shape.

How limpets get home

Limpets leave their 'home' when the tide is in and the water not too rough, also when the tide is out at night or if they are sheltered by seaweeds. They feed by rasping at the small green algae on rocks, moving around with head and tentacles protruding and swinging from side to side. Large seaweeds are not often eaten but these may be prevented from colonising areas of rock through being devoured when small. On the return journey, the limpet tends to retrace its outward track at least in part. It seems to have some kind of chemical sense for feeling its way back but there is some mystery as the limpet can get home even if its outward track is obliterated by scrubbing with detergent or chipping away stone placed in its path. The journey may cover 2 or 3 ft and limpets moved farther away rarely return home.

Cold-weather larvae

The common limpet breeds during the colder months—September to April—shedding its eggs freely into the sea. The tiny trochophore larvae hatch out about 24 hours after fertilisation. Each is $\frac{1}{120}$ in. across, with a belt of long cilia around its middle, a tuft of them on top and short cilia covering the surface between the two. A day later, the larvae become veligers with little shells. These settle and grow to about an inch long in a year. Limpets may live as long as 15 years.

△ *Rasp marks left by feeding limpet's tongue.*

▽ *Years of limpet tenancy leave their mark.*

△ *Empty slipper limpet shows its name's origin.*

Changeable sexes

Most limpets start life as males and remain this way until they are 1 in. long. As they get older, however, the proportion of females increases as the limpets reverse their sex. This has gone much further in the slipper limpet *Crepidula fornicata*, a native of North American seas which was accidentally introduced into British waters in a cargo of oysters and has since made its way round the English coast. It is not related to the common limpet, and its shell resembles a rounded slipper when laid on its back. The slipper limpet forms chains of up to eight or nine, one on top of another. It is a serious pest of oyster beds and its arrival was first noted in Britain in the 1880's and since then it has become very well established on some parts of the coast and it has spread from there to other parts of Europe. In a chain of slipper limpets, the bottom ones are females and the upper, younger ones, males: those in between are of intermediate sex. It is believed that the females release a substance into the water that causes young limpets to stay in the vicinity and to develop male characters. Young males may later move off, however, and become females, and immature individuals that settle on rock and not on females may themselves becomes females with only a short male phase, or none at all. Slipper limpets do not move about in search of food, but strain it from the water.

phylum	**Mollusca**
class	**Gastropoda**
subclass	**Prosobranchea**
order	**Archaeogastropoda**
family	**Patellidae**
genera & species	***Patella vulgata*** *common limpet* ***Patina pellucida*** *blue-rayed limpet, others*

Limpkin

The limpkin is the sole member of a family of birds that appears to be a link between the rails and the cranes. A limpkin is heron-like with long legs, a fairly long neck, a long, stout and slightly curved bill, and stands about 2 ft high. The plumage is olive-brown streaked with white.

The single species of limpkin lives in Florida and southern Georgia, then ranges from Mexico through central and southern America east of the Andes to central Argentina, as well as the West Indies.

Eerie marsh bird

The limpkin lives in freshwater marshes and swamps, sometimes in damp forests. It was once common in Georgia and Florida but was good eating and easy to shoot. Its survival is, however, now assured in sanctuaries such as the Everglades National Park in Florida, provided that the swamps are not drained. The name limpkin is derived from its strange, limping gait, as it treads gingerly across the matted swamp vegetation lifting its long toes high and twitching its tail. Limpkins swim if necessary, floating high like coots or moorhens. They rarely fly, but when they do, they take off and land vertically and fly weakly with slow steady beats. At night limpkins roost in trees where they can run among the branches with surprising agility.

Other names of the limpkin are 'crying bird' or 'wailing bird' and in Mexico it is called the 'mad widow'. These names refer to the eerie, wailing calls limpkins make, mainly at night. The calls are of three syllables and have been described as shrieks, wails and piercing cries, or as having 'a quality of unutterable sadness'. According to folklore the cries were of little boys lost for ever in the swamps.

Eating snails

Limpkins feed at wading-depth in the shallow waters of swamps and marshes. Their main food is the same large snail, the apple snail, that is the exclusive diet of the Everglade kite (p. 865). The kite can only feed on the snails when they come out to feed but the limpkin can probe for them in the mud with its long bill. The diet of snails is supplemented with other molluscs, such as freshwater mussels, worms, crayfish and occasional amphibians or reptiles, but these items are of very little importance.

The feeding grounds of limpkins are very conspicuous as they become littered with small piles of snail shells. Except when hunted limpkins are surprisingly tame and it is not too difficult to watch limpkins feeding from a boat. They feed, singly or in small flocks of up to a score. As the snails are caught they are held by the flange of the shell and carried to land or shallower water. They are lodged carefully in a crevice or in the fork of a branch with the opening upwards. The limpkin then waits patiently for the snail to relax and spears it, passing the upper half of its bill through the body between the shell and the horny operculum

or door. A quick jerk of the head detaches both operculum and shell, but instead of swallowing the body immediately, the limpkin waits for a couple of minutes before consuming it.

Precocious chicks

Nothing is known of the courtship of the limpkin but the nest is built of reeds, sticks and other plant material. It is bulky but flimsy and is lodged in tangled vines, grass clumps, a bush, or tree, sometimes as much as 17 ft up, and usually near or over water. The clutch consists of 4–8 usually 6 or 7 pale green eggs, spotted with brown. In the United States they are laid between mid-February and April and are incubated by both sexes but it is not known how long they take to hatch. The brown-black chicks can swim and run almost immediately and after a day or so leave the nest and hide nearby. They are guarded by the parents for an unknown length of time but it is known that the parents feed them after they have begun to fly. The chicks approach the parents from behind and reach forward between their legs to take the proferred snails.

Efficient snail pickers

With such a specialised diet and specialised method of feeding, both Everglade kite and limpkin must have very precarious existences. The Everglade kite, as we have seen (p. 865), is now very rare in Florida because of the draining of the swamps. The limpkin is more common and now that it is protected its numbers are increasing. In places it is abundant. The question arises as to why the limpkins can recover their numbers but not the kites. Hawks are usually well-spaced out, but Everglade kites sometimes nest in colonies, so there is not a restriction of living-room. The limpkin, of course, does exploit other food sources and it may be that it is more efficient at finding snails, being able to dig them out of the mud while the kite has to wait for them to become visible.

class	**Aves**
order	**Gruiformes**
family	**Aramidae**
genus & species	***Aramus guarauna***

Alone but for shadow and reflection, a limpkin scours the Everglades mud for snails.

Malcolm McGregor

Ling

The ling is an elongated fish of the cod family that once was an indispensable dish at the Lord Mayor's table and later furnished oil for poor people's lamps. It is often up to 6 ft long, sometimes 7 ft, with a somewhat eel-shaped body with two dorsal fins. The one in front is short, the one behind, very long, and the anal fin is long. It has a barbel on the chin. Ling, commercially valuable fish, live at depths between 300 and 600 ft where they can be fished by trawl although they are taken mainly by long line and smaller ling are caught offshore, in shallow waters, by anglers. There are three species, all in the northeast Atlantic. The common ling ranges from Iceland eastward to the Murman coast and south to the Bay of Biscay. The blue or lesser ling is in the deep water to the west of the British Isles and off Norway, at 600–3 000 ft. It and the Mediterranean ling, which is sometimes caught in the eastern Atlantic as far north as the south of Ireland, are both smaller.

A freshwater fish very like the ling is the burbot, or eel pout, the only member of the cod family living in rivers and lakes. It is shaped like a ling and is its nearest relative. It is found in England and much of Europe, including brackish waters in the Baltic.

Ling's rodent habit

Ling, like rocklings, lie still for hours with as much as possible of their bodies in contact with hard objects. According to Dr Douglas Wilson they 'press themselves into crevices, even curl around stones, following the curves as closely as possible. This may be the reason why ling is common in the neighbourhood of submerged wrecks, for they must find excellent places among the old girders on which to lie until forced by hunger to make short excursions after food.'

Some people call this the 'rodent' habit—the desire to have the back against a wall. Many people take a corner seat in a restaurant, and a mouse will run into the corner of a room, if alarmed, and sit with its hindquarters pressed into the angle of the skirting. The scientific name for this behaviour is thigmotaxis.

The food of ling is smaller fishes, especially dab, haddock and mackerel.

△ *A wide-eyed wreck haunter, the ling is a fish that likes its back to the wall; wherever possible it lies pressed along the contours of some hard object, leaving this doubtful security only to feed or spawn.*

▽ *Portrait of a burbot, the ling's freshwater relative. It is the only member of the cod family to live in lakes or rivers.*

AC Wheeler

Mother to millions

Spawning of the common ling is from March to June, or later in more northern latitudes. It takes place at depths of 600 ft or even in waters no more than 300 ft. The eggs, $\frac{1}{20}$ in. diameter, each containing a pale green oil globule, giving buoyancy, float to the surface but the fry go down into deeper water soon after hatching. When hatched the head of the baby ling is turned downwards, and so is that of the burbot hatchling. The young ling, when they reach 120–300 ft depth, grow very long pelvic fins. As time passes and the young fish grow in size these are lost. Finally the young ling reach the bottom of the sea at 3 in. length.

Ling are remarkable for the number of eggs laid. One female weighing 54 lb contained 28 361 000 eggs; another weighing 100 lb contained over 160 million.

A noble fish

Today ling is dismissed in the textbooks on fishes with the brief remark that it is a commercially valuable fish. It is mainly salted and dried. In the reign of Henry VIII things were different. When the Emperor Charles V of France visited London 'salted ling was among the principal matters provided for the entertainment of the guests.' Thomas Muffet, writing in 1655, shows that the fish was still held in high esteem. 'Ling looks perhaps for great extolling, being counted the beefe of the sea, and standing every fish day at my Lord Maiors table; yet it is nothing but a long cod, and yet hath the taste of ling: whilst it is new it is called greenfish, when it is salted it is called ling, perhaps of lyinge, because the longer it lyeth the better it is, waxing in the end as yellow as a gold noble, at which time they are worth a noble a piece.'

The high price of ling in former times can be seen in an entry for 1573, that a side of ling cost 20d whereas a side of haberdine (salted cod) cost only 8d. Yet ling had its baser uses. An oil extracted from it made a poor quality oil for lamps but a reputedly excellent remedy for rheumatism.

class	**Osteichthyes**
order	**Gadiformes**
family	**Gadidae**
genera & species	***Molva molva*** *common ling* **M. dypterygia** *blue ling* **M. macrophthalma** *Mediterranean ling* **Lota lota** *burbot*

Linnet

Linnets are like the famous Scarlet Pimpernel in the way they can be all around and yet remain unseen, or at least undetected. This is partly because of their shyness, partly the result of their colouring. About the size of a house sparrow, 5¼ in. long, the male has a chestnut brown back and is fawn shading to almost white on the underside, with a greyish brown head mottled or streaked with darker brown. The flight feathers and tail have white edges. This is his winter plumage and then the bill is horn coloured. By the spring he boasts a crimson crown and breast, the beak then being lead-coloured. The crimson patches appear as the grey ends of the feathers are worn away. The female is slightly smaller than the male. She lacks the crimson of the male and her plumage is duller and greyer and the dark streaks on her head and breast are more obvious.

*These differences in colour have led to the bird being given different names: brown, red and grey linnet. The name 'linnet' is from the Old French and is based on **lin** (or flax) presumably because the bird ate the seeds of flax. It has also been applied to related finches. The greenfinch has been called green linnet. The twite is the mountain linnet, and a North American siskin **Spinus pinus** is called the pine linnet.*

The linnet itself ranges over Europe, except for the extreme north, northwest Africa, southwest Asia and part of Central Asia, from sea level up to the tree line.

Second to the nightingale?

Linnets are found in almost any place where there are bushes or trees; in copses, plantations, hedges, gardens with shrubberies or uncultivated land with rank vegetation, such as gorse or bramble. In winter, however, when linnets come together in flocks they move across arable land and stubble fields, or they may search the birches in marshland or the alders beside rivers in company with siskins.

Linnets are noted for their song. One 17th century writer put the linnet second only to the nightingale. Several males may sometimes be seen in one bush singing in a chorus which does not carry far but is pleasing and musical. Some of the high notes are flute-like, some of the low notes are harp-like. It seems that linnets do not sing to mark out a territory, and they may sing while perched high on a bush, on the ground or on the wing. Formerly linnets were valued as cage birds and there was a belief that a linnet crossed with a canary produced an even better song than either of the parent species. In fact, the song of a linnet is mainly learned, not inborn, so it could not be affected much by inheritance.

Seeds of danger

Typically seed eaters taking small seeds of garden weeds, but more especially flax, hemp and brassicas such as turnips and cabbage linnets will also take berries and oats in winter. They eat some insects and the young are fed on caterpillars, fly larvae, small beetles and spiders. A remarkable observation was recorded by Julian M Langford, in *British Birds* for November 1962. When ringing linnets in September and October he found several blinded in one eye from the hooked seeds of bur-marigold. As he remarked 'it seemed curious that they should expose themselves to such a source of danger' and suggests the damage may have been done when they were suddenly disturbed and took hasty flight. It may be one of the drawbacks to their shyness.

Close neighbours

The breeding season begins in April and eggs may be laid any time up to August. The nest is built of grass, bents, sometimes fine twigs, and moss lined with wool, hair vegetable down or feathers. It is sited in a bush or shrub, not more than a few feet from the ground. In it 4—6 pale bluish eggs with spots, occasionally streaks, of purple-red are laid. These are incubated for 10—12 days by the hen mainly, the male relieving her for only short periods. The young are fed by both parents for 11—12 days, and there may be 2 or 3 broods a year.

Linnets tend to nest in groups, with several nests a few feet from each other. Normally they nest well away from houses but will occasionally build in a bush beside a porch or near a window. Such nests help to show how shy linnets can be because even occupants of the house, using a window as a hide, have difficulty in watching the bird on the nest or flying from or into it.

Hidden talents

Goldfinches are renowned for the way they can pull strings to get food (see p 1063). Crows and jays have been seen to do the same, so have siskins, redpolls and tits. These will not only pull strings but will pull food, such as catkins towards them, using one foot, while perched with the other. Linnets are close relatives of siskins and redpolls and it has been suggested that the reason they do not generally do these things is because they are mainly ground feeders. Therefore they have no instinct to use a foot to get food and they have neither the incentive nor the experience to guide them into doing so. This is surprising since linnets and redpolls often feed together in birches and alders. Indeed, 15 years ago, Derek Goodwin, an experienced British ornithologist, described seeing linnets taking seeds from the catkins of birch. They drew the catkins towards them with the beak, then held them with the left foot to remove the seeds, just as skilfully as a redpoll or a goldfinch.

class	**Aves**
order	**Passeriformes**
family	**Fringillidae**
genus & species	**Acanthis cannabina**

An attentive father feeding his hungry brood.

Linsang

The linsang is probably the most slender member of the family Viverridae, which includes the mongooses, civets, genets and related species. The family itself stands between the cat family on the one hand and the weasel family on the other. All viverrids belong to the Old World tropics and subtropics. There are two species, the larger of which is the banded linsang.

The banded linsang is $2\frac{1}{2}$ ft in total length, of which nearly half is tail, and weighs just over $1\frac{1}{2}$ lb. Its body is long and slender, its legs short and its head slender with a sharp snout. The claws are retractile, those on the forepaws being sheathed like a cat, those on the hindfeet being protected by lobes of skin. The eyes are large and the big ears are delicate and sensitive. The fur is short and thick, and feels like velvet. Its ground colour is whitish to brownish grey with six broad irregular brownish-black bands across the back, a stripe of similar colour along each side of the neck and the lower flanks and outsides of the legs are marked with dark spots. The tail is ringed white and blackish-brown. The slightly smaller spotted linsang has a ground colour of either pale brown or orange-buff with rows of black spots on the back and flanks. The tail is also ringed.

◁ *Eyes alight, body low on the ground, the typical pose of a stalking banded linsang.*

The banded linsang ranges from Tenasserim, Burma, through Malaya to Java, Sumatra and Borneo. The spotted linsang is found from Nepal through Assam to Vietnam. The name 'linsang' is Javanese but it has also been applied to a West African species of viverrid **Poiana richardsoni** which looks and behaves like a genet (p. 1011) and should be so described.

Feeds like any flesh-eater

Linsangs are solitary nocturnal prowlers, resting most of the day in hollows in trees. They are agile in climbing trees but spend much time on the ground, in both situations hunting lizards, frogs, small mammals, small birds and insects. Fish may be taken at times; birds' eggs are broken with a blow of the forepaw and the contents lapped up. Information on their breeding is scanty. It is

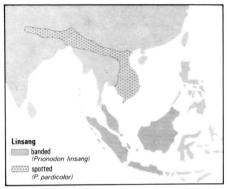

Linsang
▤ banded
(*Prionodon linsang*)
▦ spotted
(*P. pardicolor*)

believed they have two litters a year, one in February, the other in August. The 2 or 3 babies are raised in a nest of sticks and leaves in hollow trees, in a hole in the ground or between the buttress roots of large trees.

Acting like a snake

When a fox is stalking prey, or even when trying to elude hounds it can drop its body between its shoulder-blades so it is running almost belly to ground. With its head and neck stretched horizontally forwards the fox can almost disappear into a furrow in a ploughed field. The genets, civets and mongooses have carried this a stage further because their bodies are longer and their legs shorter, and they seem to be able to stretch the neck until it is half as long again. The linsang has the edge even on the genets and mongooses. As it slips rapidly through the grass, body slung low between its short legs, slender pointed head straining forward on a long neck and with its tail held stiffly and horizontally to the rear it looks more like a somewhat plump snake gliding towards its prey.

class	**Mammalia**
order	**Carnivora**
family	**Viverridae**
genus & species	*Prionodon linsang* banded linsang **P. pardicolor** spotted linsang

▽ *Graceful hunter, the alert spotted linsang looks for potential prey. This beautiful mammal is often mistaken for a poisonous snake as its slender body moves through the undergrowth.*

Okapia

South African Tourist Corporation

Lion

Lions were once common throughout southern Europe and southern Asia eastwards to northern and central India and over the whole of Africa. The last lion died in Europe between 80 – 100 AD. By 1884 the only lions left in India were in the Gir forest where only a dozen were left, and they were probably extinct elsewhere in southern Asia, for example, in Iran and Iraq, soon after that date. Since the beginning of this century the Gir lions have been protected and a few years ago they were estimated to number 300. The last census, taken in 1968, put the figure at about 170. Lions have been wiped out in northern Africa, and in southern Africa, outside the Kruger Park.

The total length of a lion may be up to 9 ft of which 3 ft is tail, the height at the shoulder is $3\frac{1}{2}$ ft and the weight up to 550 lb. The lioness is smaller. The coat is tawny; the mane of the male is tawny to black, dense or thin, and maneless lions occur in some districts. The mane grows on the head, neck and shoulders and may extend to the belly.

◁ Shady business: lioness evades the heat.
▷ An aspiring lion claims a higher position.
▽ Pride of the bush: lionesses with their cubs.
◁◁ Romantic yearnings? Lion in the dusk.

Sally Anne Thompson

Gerald Cubitt

Bavaria

Prides and the hunting urge

Lions live in open country with scrub, spreading trees or reedbeds. The only sociable member of the cat family, they live in groups known as prides of up to 20, exceptionally 37, made up of one or more mature lions and a number of lionesses with juveniles or cubs. Members of a pride will co-operate in hunting, to stalk or ambush prey, and they combine for defence. The roar is usually not used when hunting although lions have been heard to roar and to give a grunting roar to keep in touch when stalking. A lion is capable of speeds of up to 40 mph but only in short bursts. It can make standing jumps of up to 12 ft high and leaps of 40 ft. Lions will not normally climb trees but lionesses may jump onto low branches to sun themselves and they as well as lions will sometimes climb trees to reach a kill cached in a fork by a leopard. There is one record of a lioness chasing a leopard, apparently with the intent to kill it, into a tree, but she was foiled by the leopard going into the slender top branches which failed to bear the lioness's weight.

Not wholly carnivorous

Although strongly carnivorous lions take fallen fruit at times. Normally, in addition to the protein, fat, carbohydrate and mineral salts, lions get their vitamins from the entrails of the herbivores they kill. Typically, lions first eat the entrails and hindquarters working forward to the head. In captivity, lions flourish best and breed successfully when vitamins are added to a raw meat diet. Although lionesses often make the kill the lions eat first (hence, 'the lion's share') the lionesses coming next and the cubs last. In general, antelopes and zebra form the bulk of lions' kills but almost anything animal will be taken, from cane rats to elephant, hippopotamus, giraffe, buffalo and even ostrich.

A survey in the Kruger Park showed that in order of numbers killed the prey-species were: wildebeest, impala, zebra, waterbuck, kudu, giraffe, buffalo. A later survey showed a preference descending through waterbuck, wildebeest, kudu, giraffe, sable, tsessebe, zebra, buffalo, reedbuck, impala. When age or injury prevents a lion catching agile prey it may turn to porcupines and smaller rodents, to sheep

▽ *Violence afoot: hampered by the water around them, a pair of paddling lions make the opening moves of a soggy trial of strength.*

Photos by A Visage: Jacana

and goats, or turn man-killer, taking children and women more particularly. Maneating can become a habit, however; once a small group of lions at Tsavo held up the building of the Uganda railway through their attacks on the labourers. Dogs may be killed but not eaten.

Exaggerated story of strength

A favourite story is of a lion entering a compound, killing a cow and jumping with it over the stockade. R Hewitt Ivy argues in *African Wild Life* for June 1960 that this is impossible. His explanation is that lions visiting a cattle compound do not all go inside. Possibly one leaps the fence, makes a kill and drags it under the fence to those waiting outside. Should the cattle panic and one leap the fence it will be pulled down by the rest of the pride outside and there eaten.

The lion hunts in silence and it is the lioness that most often kills the prey. The usual method of killing is to leap at the prey and break the neck with the front paws. Alternatively a lion may seize it by the throat with its teeth or throttle it with the forepaws, on the throat or nostrils. Another method is to leap at the hindquarters and pull the prey down. A lion will kill a hippopotamus by scoring its flesh with the claws in a running battle. Lions will kill and eat a crocodile and will also eat carrion, especially if it is fresh, and lion will eat dead lion. An old story tells of the lion's habit of lashing itself into a fury with a spur on the end of its tail, in order to drive itself to attack. Some lions do have what appears to be a claw at the tip of the tail. But this is only the last one or two vertebrae in the tail out of place, due to injury.

Natural control of populations

Lions begin to breed at 2 years but reach their prime at 5 years. The males are polygamous. There is a good deal of roaring before and during mating, and fights with intruding males may take place. Gestation is 105–112 days, the number of cubs in a litter is 2–5, born blind and with a spotted coat. The eyes open at 6 days, weaning is at 3 months after which the lioness teaches the cubs to hunt, which they can do for themselves at a year old. There is a high death rate among cubs because they feed last, so suffering from a diet deficiency, especially of vitamins. This serves as a natural check

▽ *On firmer ground. The skirmish begins as one lion lumbers up onto his rear legs and lunges at his equally cumbersome opponent.*

on numbers. Should numbers fall unduly in a district—as when lions are hunted by man or culled in national parks—prey is more easily killed and there is more food to spare. Lionesses will then kill for their cubs and then the cubs eat first. This richer diet makes for a high survival rate among the cubs, so restoring the balance in the population number.

Dangers for the King of Beasts

There are no natural enemies as such, apart from man, but lions are prone to casualties, especially the young and inexperienced. A zebra stallion may lash out and kick a lion in the teeth, after which the lion may have to hunt small game. The sable antelope is more than a match for a single lion and other antelopes have sometimes impaled lions on their horns. A herd of buffalo may

1 An affectionate nudge from mother.
2 Lioness casually accepts a mother's duty.
3 Drink up! One lioness remains on watch.
4 That drowsy after dinner feeling? In fact lions sleep for up to 18 hours a day.
5 Safety in numbers for grazing wildebeest.
▷ Reversal of the roles? It is usually the lioness who does the hunting but here a lion proudly drags his kill to cover.
▽ Plan of campaign: lion's strategy observed in Kruger Park. Detecting wildebeest, 16 lions split into three parties. During a campaign of almost human organisation the leader kept the group alert with tail flicking signals. The wildebeest veered in time but almost met their doom in the ambush party.

trample a lion or toss it from one set of horns to another until it is dead, although two lions will overcome one large buffalo. One female giraffe attacked a lioness trying to kill her calf. Using hoofs of fore and hindlegs, as well as beating the lioness with her neck, she severely mauled her—and chased the lioness away over a distance of 100 yards. This is a better performance than a rhinoceros can manage. A lion will kill rhino up to three-quarters grown.

Start counting . . .

How does one take a census of lions in a forest, as in the Gir Forest? First, a rough count was made by taking note over a month of the number of lion kills. Second, for 2 days a count was made of all pug marks. Third, 100 buffalo calves were placed at

different points throughout the forest—horrible thought! 'It was assumed that within two or three days nearly all the lions would have found a bait and would remain with it for the remainder of the five-day enumeration.' The totals from the three methods were 160, 166 and 162—a fair agreement which indicates a reasonable accuracy in the count. Allowing for numbers missed Mr Oza, Deputy Forest Minister of Gujarat State, estimates a population of about 177 lions.

class	**Mammalia**
order	**Carnivora**
family	**Felidae**
genus & species	***Panthera leo*** *lion*

Popperfoto

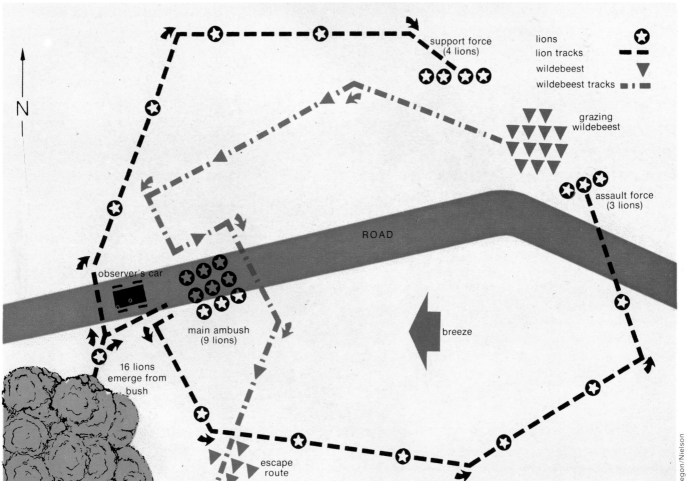

N

lions ⭐
lion tracks ▬ ▬
wildebeest ▼
wildebeest tracks ▬ ▪ ▬

support force
(4 lions)

grazing
wildebeest

assault force
(3 lions)

ROAD

observer's car

main ambush
(9 lions)

breeze

16 lions
emerge from
bush

escape
route

Legon/Nielson

Little auk

The little auk or dovekie is the smallest of the Atlantic auks, only 8 in. long. Its bill is short, almost finchlike; it looks very different from other auks but in flight, or from a distance, it may be mistaken for a young guillemot or razorbill. The plumage is black with white underparts and white patches on the wings. A small white patch over the eye, seen only at close quarters, gives it a comical appearance. In the winter the upper part of the breast, throat and sides of the head become white.

Little auks breed in the Arctic, around the coasts of Greenland, Jan Mayen, Bear Island, Svalbard, Novaya Zemlya, Franz Josef Land and Grimsey, off Iceland. They range south into the North Atlantic to the coasts of the British Isles in the east to those of the New England States in the west. Occasionally little auks come farther south, as far as the Mediterranean, off the Azores and off Cuba.

Wrecks of auks

Little auks are perhaps the most abundant birds of the North Atlantic, their rivals being Brünnich's guillemots. In temperate regions they are seen offshore in large flocks but these are not half as spectacular as the immense numbers that haunt the colonies on the cliffs around the Arctic seas. The cliffs of Greenland and other Arctic islands may be hundreds or even thousands of feet high and they are packed with guillemots, razorbills and other sea birds, as well as with little auks that make their nests on the narrow ledges or among rocks and scree. Surrounding the cliffs are clouds of birds flying to and from their nests while the air is filled with their twittering. Charles Elton has described the scene as being like 'a vast opera house, packed with crowds of people in white shirt-fronts and black tails, all whispering comments on each other and rustling their programmes.' The little auks are not as obvious as the other seabirds because they nest in crevices, but one colony, at Scoresby Sound on the east coast of

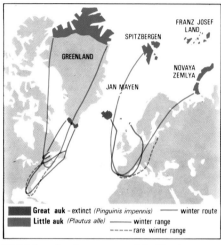

Great auk – extinct (*Pinguinis impennis*) ⎯⎯ winter route
Little auk (*Plautus alle*) ⎯⎯ winter range
- - - - rare winter range

▽ *Little auks, the sparrows of the North Atlantic, are retreating further north every year as the edge of the ice pack recedes.*

Greenland, contains an estimated 5 million little auk nests, while there are uncounted millions in the colony at Cape York.

Occasionally flocks of little auks are blown inland by gales and many perish. These 'wrecks', as they are called, occur when the little auks are caught on a lee shore and are unable to manoeuvre out to sea against the wind. The stranded birds turn up on ponds and lakes, on roads and fields or in gardens. Those that can land on water may be lucky enough to be able to take off when the weather improves but most die of starvation and exhaustion or fall prey to cats, dogs, foxes, crows and other predators.

Retreating from warmth

The food of little auks is mainly crustaceans such as amphipods, copepods and northern species of krill. Small fishes, worms and other planktonic animals are also caught. Like the related guillemots, little auks chase their prey underwater, swimming with their wings.

The main feeding grounds of the little auks are along the edge of the pack ice where there are concentrations of planktonic animals. The importance of this area as a source of food is shown by the effect that the general retreat of the pack ice has had on the populations of little auks in Iceland. In 1903 there were an estimated 200–300 pairs nesting on Grimsey; by 1949 there were 19 birds left. This reduction is almost certainly due to the distance between the pack ice and the colony increasing because the North Atlantic is warming up, so making it difficult for the little auks to collect enough food for their young.

Nesting in crevices

Little auks nest in crevices of worn rock faces, among the stones or scree slopes or in the talus—the pile of boulders that accumulates at the base of a cliff. The nests are usually high on the cliffs and may be found on inland cliff faces some distance from the sea. Sometimes the little auks dig out the soil among the stones to make a better hole and they then make a nest of pebbles about 1 yd from the entrance.

A single pale-blue egg is laid in late June and hatched 3–4 weeks later after incubation by both parents, who feed the chick on plankton eight or nine times a day, bringing the food to the nest in cheek-pouches. The chick leaves the nest when 29 days old. Unlike a young guillemot, it can fly well from the start, as is necessary when it is brought up on inland cliffs.

Young are vulnerable

Seabirds that nest on cliffs are safe from many enemies but eggs and chicks of little auks are taken by Arctic skuas and glaucous gulls which can land and forage among the rocks. The glaucous gulls also kill the young little auks as they set off on their first flight. Arctic foxes also hunt on the more accessible scree slopes and cliff ledges, and in Greenland men take both chicks and adults and store them for winter use.

Death of the great auk

The great auk, or garefowl, was more closely related to guillemots than to the little auk. The size of a goose, the great auk was flightless and was the original penguin, the name

Natural History Museum

△ *Grounded—permanently. The great auk, standing 30 in. high, was the only flightless bird in the northern hemisphere, but June 1844 saw the last pair slaughtered.*
▽ *One-way traffic: these tiny little auks, only 8 in. long, return in their thousands each spring to breed well within the Arctic.*

being later given to the familiar flightless birds of the southern hemisphere. Once great auks bred freely on islands such as St Kilda off Scotland, Eldey off Iceland, the Magdalen Islands in the Gulf of St Lawrence and Funk Island in Newfoundland. From time immemorial, man caught great auks for food, often when they came near the mainland during winter. Between the 16th and 18th centuries, however, they were slaughtered on a large scale by people living near the breeding grounds or by crews needing to revictual their ships. As the great auks were unable to fly it was simple to drive them to the shore, then up a gangplank and into a boat.

By the 18th century great auks were rare, even in Newfoundland where they had been very abundant. In the first half of the 19th century they were finally killed off. They were forgotten by the islanders of St Kilda, who at one time used great auk fat as a remedy for aches and pains. Then, in 1840, a straggler appeared on the island and was clubbed by two islanders who thought it was a witch. The last great auks ever seen were two which were killed, and their egg smashed, on the island of Eldey in the first week of June 1844.

class	**Aves**
order	**Charadriiformes**
family	**Alcidae**
genera & species	***Plautus alle*** *little auk* ***Pinguinus impennis*** *great auk*

G Ruppell

Llama

If the name of this South American humpless camel were given its correct pronunciation 'yama' we could avoid confusion with the spiritual head of the Tibetans. The llama has long been domesticated. Its wild ancestor was probably the guañaco, the other wild camel of South America being the vicuña. The alpaca was probably also derived from the same wild ancestor.

The guañaco ranges from North Peru to the southern plains of Patagonia. It is nearly 6 ft in head and body length, including a fairly long neck, and its tail is nearly 10 in. long. It stands nearly 4 ft at the shoulder, 5 ft to the top of the head, and it weighs up to 210 lb. Its woolly coat is tawny to brown and the head is grey. It lives in herds of a few females with one male, but there are leaderless herds of males up to 200 strong. For defence guañacos rely on speed, up to 40 mph, and they readily take to water. Mating takes place in August and September the single young being born 10–11 months later. It runs swiftly soon after birth and is weaned at 6–12 weeks.

The vicuña is slightly smaller and weighs only 100 lb. It ranges from north Peru to the northern parts of Chile, keeping more to the mountains, usually above 14 000 ft. It is up to 3 ft at the shoulder, with a light brown coat and yellowish-red bib.

The chief interest in what is sometimes called the llamoid group – the llama, alpaca, guañaco and vicuña – lies in the history of their domestication and the relationships between the four animals, which are still unsolved. When in 1531 the Spanish conquistadores overran the Inca Empire in the high Andes they found the llama and alpaca both numerous as domesticated animals. The llama is larger than the wild guañaco, weighing up to 300 lb. Its coat is of a long, dense fine wool. It was and still is used mainly as a beast of burden, with an uncertain temper, a greater tendency to spit than a camel and to bite. The alpaca, smaller than the llama, was selectively bred for its coat which makes a finer quality wool than that of any other animal. It is much longer also and was formerly woven into robes used by Inca royalty.

Which ancestor?

Bones agreeing with those of both the llama and the guañaco have been unearthed in human settlements of a date which suggests that their domestication goes back 4 500 years. It may have been even earlier than this, so we can only guess at their wild ancestors and in this there is a sharp difference of opinion among the few zoologists who have made the study. The first to do so was O Antonius, the Austrian

◁ *Old fashioned? Life in the Andes and for the llamas has changed little since the Incas.*

△ *The child of the year: llamas produce only one offspring each year.*

palaeontologist who, in 1922, argued that the llama was derived from the guañaco and the alpaca from the vicuña. Thirty years later, several others re-examined the arguments and decided Antonius was wrong, and that a study of the skulls more especially showed that the two domesticated forms were both derived from one wild ancestor, the guañaco. Both schools of thought have their followers today, and the matter cannot be settled by breeding. The llama and the alpaca interbreed to produce fertile offspring, which suggests strongly they belong to one species. In captivity both the guañaco and the vicuña interbreed to give fertile offspring, which is unusual for distinct species. There is, however, one marked difference between the two wild forms. The vicuña is less easy to tame because of its shyness than the guañaco, although the Jesuits in South America showed that it could be domesticated. There are other views on this matter. One is that the alpaca may have been derived from hybrids between the wild vicuña and the domesticated llama. The other is that possibly both llama and vicuña were bred from a wild species that long ago became extinct.

Life at the top

Although today the motorised vehicle tends to oust the llama as a pack animal it is still of prime importance to the people living high in the Andes. It and the other llamoids are fitted for life at these heights because their haemoglobin can take in more oxygen than that of other mammals and their red corpuscles have a longer lifespan – 235 days as against the 100 days of human blood corpuscles. Apart from their use for transport – and a llama usually refuses a load of more than 50 lb – llamas provide meat, wool for clothing, hides for sandals and fat for candles. Its wool when braided is used for ropes and its dung is dried and used for fuel. Once a llama is dead little is wasted from its carcase.

Persecution for tourism

Besides making use of the domesticated llamoids the wild species have long been corraled, sheared and then released. In the modern world, with the development of tourism, there has grown up a big demand for products from these animals. One result is a heavy persecution of the wild species so they are much more rare than formerly and fears are being expressed that they may become extinct. As an example of wasteful manufacture a vicuña bedcover displayed for sale to tourists was made up of the skins from at least 40 animals.

Scientists kept out

It is a little surprising that we should have so little information on the biology of animals that have been domesticated for over 4 000 years, or of their wild relations. It is much the same story for the South American fauna as a whole and it is explainable, at least partly, by the early history of the Spanish Conquest. Francisco Pizarro, who defeated the Incas, is said to have sent back false reports of this new-found land to prevent the Spanish crown from realising the full extent of its wealth. In any case, the Spanish authorities had their own reasons for not making public the full potential of their colonies. As a result permission to enter the interior of South America was strictly withheld until towards the end of the 18th century, when the first naturalists were allowed in – and these 200 lost years have not yet been overtaken.

class	**Mammalia**
order	**Artiodactyla**
family	**Camelidae**
genus & species	***Lama pacos*** *alpaca* ***Guañacoe*** *guañaco* ***L. glama*** *llama* ***Vicugna vicugna*** *vicuña*

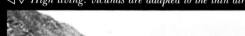

△ *Chins up: llamas ear-marked for a life of service.*
◁△ *Llama: domesticated but never tamed.*
◁▽ *High living: vicunas are adapted to the thin air.*

Leggy wool bags: guanacos in Whipsnade Zoo.
Alpacas are bred for their fine quality wool.
End of the road: llamas from the silver mines unload.

Loach

The two dozen species of loaches and spiny loaches live in the fresh waters of Europe and Asia, including the Malayan Archipelago, as well as a small area in Morocco and one in Ethiopia. They are small, seldom more than 1 ft long, and while a few have a fairly normal fish-shape apart from a flattened under-surface, most are worm-shaped. Most of them have a conspicuous pattern of dark bands on the body or it may be broken up, or otherwise altered, until only a marbling remains. They have small scales in the skin. There are three or four pairs of barbels around the toothless mouth which is set back beneath the snout. The single dorsal fin, the anal fin and the paired fins are all much the same size. The spined loach is named for a spine, which may fork at its tip, below and in front of the eye.

*Except for three species, the stone loach, spined loach and weatherfish, all belong to southern and southeast Asia, and these include two well known to aquarists, the coolie loach and the clown or tiger loach. The common name coolie is derived from the scientific name **Acanthophthalmus kuhlii**. The most colourful of the family is the clown or tiger loach, brilliant orange-red with velvet black bars.*

Automatic air-conditioning

Loaches are bottom-living. Those living in streams have rounded bodies, somewhat flattened from above down in some species, while those living in still water have bodies flattened from side to side. They use their barbels to hunt for food—mainly insect larvae and worms—and some species burrow into the sand or mud at the bottom, either to escape enemies or to pass the winter. Loaches sometimes eat algae and were often kept by aquarists to clear the aquarium walls of green coatings. Their usual method of feeding, however, is to comb the surface of the sand or mud, swallowing edible particles and passing solid grains out through the gills.

Two features of the behaviour of loaches are particularly impressive: the way they breathe and the way they react to changes in the weather. Loaches have gills, and a swimbladder whose front part—in some species at least—is enclosed in a bony capsule. Many loaches breathe through the intestine. When the water becomes impure they come to the surface and gulp air which they swallow. They also gulp air if the pond dries up and, burying themselves in the mud, wait for rain. The wall of the hind end of the intestine is rich in small blood vessels and works like a lung, taking in oxygen and giving out carbon dioxide, the spent air being expelled through the vent.

Experiments in aquaria show a direct relation between the air gulping and a rising temperature of the water. The warmer the water the less oxygen it holds. At 5°C/41°F a loach breathes solely through

△ *An affectionate pair of clown loaches. This orange coloured loach with its velvet black bars is a hardy species renowned for its habit of uprooting rank vegetation. It has been known to live for 25 years in captivity.*
▷ *With its sensitive barbels extended the stone loach hunts for food. A toothless fish, the loach eats mainly insect larvae and worms and occasionally algae. Obviously a useful fish to keep aquarium walls clean.*

its gills. At 10°C/50°F one bubble of air is swallowed every 2 hours. At 15°C/59°F five bubbles are swallowed in an hour. At 25°C/77°F ten bubbles are swallowed an hour. If, however, a loach is placed in water that has been boiled to drive out oxygen, and is then cooled to 25°C/77°F it will swallow 67 bubbles an hour, coming to the surface every minute or so to gulp.

Switch from gills to lungs

In some species most of the intestine is used as a lung. This is true of the stone loach and spiny loach as well as the weatherfish, an Indian species *Lepidocephalus guntea* and a Chinese species, the mud loach *Misgurnus anguillicaudatus*. After gulping air, the Indian loach turns a somersault, at the same time driving out the spent air through its vent. A stream of 8–12 bubbles are ejected with force producing a distinct clicking sound. When these bubbles are collected and analysed they are found to contain only a small percentage of carbon dioxide, the rest being nitrogen and some oxygen. In fact, most of the carbon dioxide is got rid of through the gills.

The Chinese loach is remarkable because it has a seasonal lung. It uses gills only in winter, when there is more oxygen in the cold water, but in summer it becomes an air-gulper. Moreover, as the fish resumes its gill-breathing the 'lung' part of the intestine reverts to digestive tissue.

Famous for fecundity

Although loaches have been popular aquarium fishes little is known of the breeding habits of most of them. They have only occasionally spawned in captivity and accounts of what happens are conflicting. One writer has spoken of the eggs being laid on sand, another in a bubble nest. More is known about the stone loach, which has a reputation of being a prolific breeder and

in Shakespeare's Henry IV there is the phrase 'breeds fleas like a loach', which is supposed to refer to its fecundity. Izaak Walton claimed that the loach is usually full of spawn and breeds three times a year. It spawns indiscriminately on stones and pebbles in April to May, the eggs being laid at night. The eggs are large for so small a fish, $\frac{1}{25}$ in. diameter, sticky and numerous. They hatch in 8–11 days, the fry lying on the bottom at first and beginning to feed at 8–10 days after hatching.

Weather prophets

Several species of fishes are supposed to foretell weather changes. One of the most famous is a loach known in continental Europe as the weatherfish, but other loaches are said to do much the same. The name 'loach' is said to be from the French *locher*, to fidget, and, loaches are said to grow restless 24 hours before the approach of a thunderstorm. They are said to be sensitive to changes in barometric pressure although there have been no experiments to test this. A theory put forward in 1895 is that the Weberian ossicles function as a barometer. These bones connect a fish's swimbladder with its inner ear.

class	**Osteichthyes**
order	**Cypriniformes**
family	**Cobitidae**
genera & species	***Botia macracanthus*** *clown loach* ***Cobitis taenia*** *spined loach* ***Misgurnus fossilis*** *weatherfish* ***Noemacheilus barbatulus*** *stone loach* *others*

Lobster

The common lobster of Europe is very like the crayfish (p. 699), but it differs in being larger, sometimes weighing 10 lb and even 15 lb has been recorded. Also it is marine and predominantly blue in colour (going red when boiled). Another difference is in the pincers. One is very large and heavy, and is used for crushing, the other is smaller and toothed for holding and tearing food. There are also small pincers on the first two of the four pairs of walking legs. The American east coast lobster is like the European in all but a few minor details. The largest on record weighed 44½ lb and its body alone was 2 ft long, but on both sides of the Atlantic the average size of lobsters has diminished greatly as a result of being fished. Few now live long enough to approach this size.

The many other kinds of lobster include, in European waters, the smaller Norway lobster or 'Dublin prawn', up to 8 in., a delicate flesh colour and the source of scampi, and the spiny lobster, crawfish or langouste, which grows up to 18 in. Spiny lobsters lack large pinching claws but have protective spines on the body and long spiny antennae, like South Sea Island maces, that can be used to repel enemies. At the bases of the antennae of the spiny lobster of the American west coast are sound-producing organs that the lobster uses when molested. Each is made up of a flap that plays back and forth on a smooth ridge. Its purpose is not understood; perhaps it scares off fish. It is not yet known whether or not lobsters can hear water- or air-borne sounds.

Both the common European and the Norway lobsters range along the European coasts from Norway to the Mediterranean. The common lobster lives on rocky coasts, venturing up the shore only occasionally between tidemarks, especially in summer. The Norway lobster is trawled from muddy bottoms in deeper water while the spiny lobster is a more southerly species of rocky coasts. It is more important as food in the Mediterranean region than elsewhere.

Burrowers and hoarders

Lobsters move over the seabed on four pairs of walking legs, often propelled forwards by the beating of the swimmerets under their abdomens. In addition, to escape a predator they may dart suddenly backwards by flicking forward under their bodies their jointed abdomens, which end in tail-fans. The common lobster, active particularly at night, spends much of its time with its long sensory antennae protruding from the safety of a rocky crevice or a burrow it has dug itself. It eats a variety of animal matter, living and dead—like the stale fish used to bait lobster pots—and sometimes its own kind. It also eats a small amount of seaweed and eelgrass. The food is shredded into tiny pieces by a pair of mandibles helped by

△ Live scampi! Pincers outstretched the Norway lobster is ready for action.

▽ Sandy recluse. The pretty blue European lobster sits quietly in shallow water.

▽ Halt, who goes there! A passing sea bream casts a wary eye at the raised antenna of the spiny lobster. The sea perch, unabashed with the little scene, carries on its way.

Klaus Paysan

Bavaria

Popperfoto

the three pairs of maxillipeds, which together make up its 'jaws', but is further broken up in the gizzard. Lobsters sometimes store food in their burrows and there is an account in *Nature* for 1877 of a lobster standing guard over a dead flounder buried under the gravel in an aquarium at Rothesay and digging it up at intervals to eat a bit more of it.

A glutton for chalk

The female common lobster begins breeding when she is about 8 in. long, and after that she spawns once every two years, in July to August. In mating, she lies on her back while the male places, with specially modified swimmerets, a packet of sperms in a receptacle between the last pairs of her walking legs. The thousands of dark green eggs she lays are cemented onto her swimmerets and there remain, protected and aerated, for 10–11 months. She is then said to be 'in berry' and the law forbids the sale of females in berry. The young hatch as shrimp-like 'mysis' larvae about ⅓ in. long, with large eyes and no swimmerets. For the next few months they swim in the surface waters, then sink to the bottom when about ½ in long.

They grow by periodic moulting of the hard external skeleton, about eight times during the first year, fewer during the next two years, and only once (female) or twice (male) a year after the third year. The skeleton is heavily impregnated with lime salts and before a moult much of the lime is re-absorbed into the body for re-use. It is stored temporarily in the liver and as two large 'stones' in the stomach. After a moult, a lobster develops a craving for calcium carbonate which it may devour in the form of its own cast skin and of the shells of other animals such as molluscs or sea urchins. If other sources are denied it, a lobster may turn cannibal. Even with adequate supplies of calcium carbonate the shell takes about six weeks to become fully hardened and during this time the lobster must remain in the protection of its home if it is not to fall prey to sharks, skates or cod, the last of these being its main enemy.

Some idea of the proportions of eggs laid can be gained from the following figures for the American east coast lobster. A female 8 in. long lays 5 000, one 10 in. long lays 10 000, and a female 17 in. long lays 63 000. The largest number recorded was 97 440.

Self-mutilation

If you catch a lobster by one of its walking legs or more especially by a claw, it is likely you will be left with just that in your hand while the rest of the animal escapes. It is not that the limbs are brittle, but there is a special reflex mechanism for sacrificing a trapped member for the preservation of the whole, as when a lizard casts its tail. The break occurs at a predetermined breaking plane visible as an encircling groove towards the base of the limb and there is a special muscle that causes the fracture, bending the limb in such a way as to put great strain on the plane of weakness. The reaction is automatic, as when we blink our eyes, and never involves the brain, only the nerve centre of that particular limb.

The wound is very much less than would come from breakage elsewhere on the limb, for no muscles cross the breaking plane.

Moreover, the hard skeleton turns inwards here, and there is a membrane over the exposed area, perforated to let nerves and blood vessels pass through. Loss of the lobster's blue blood is minimised since it clots in the wound and seals it.

Limbs lost either in this way or by other means are replaced when the lobster next moults—in miniature at first, but growing at successive moults until they reach normal size. Moulting may occur sooner than usual, for example, within 150 days, but without the normal increase in body size, if more than three legs have been lost. It may happen that the small claw is regenerated inappropriately as a second large one, or vice versa, so destroying the normal asymmetry of the lobster. More curious is the fact that if one of the stalked eyes is removed, it may be replaced at the moult by an extra antennule, complete with at least some of the connections to the brain that an antennule should have.

phylum	**Arthropoda**
class	**Crustacea**
order	**Decapoda**
super family	**Nephropsidea**
genus & species	**Homarus vulgaris** *European lobster* **H. americanus** *American east coast lobster* **Nephrops norvegicus** *Norway lobster*
super family	**Scyllaridea**
genus	**Palinurus**

▽ *The long arm of defence: the long antennae and spines of the spiny lobster help to protect it from its enemies*

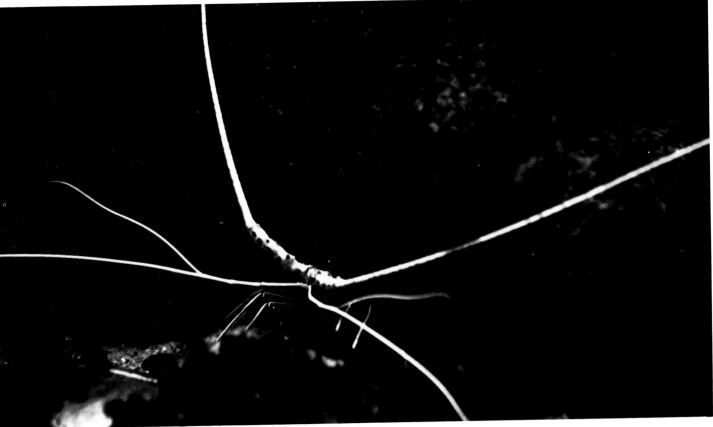

Russ Kinne: Photo Res

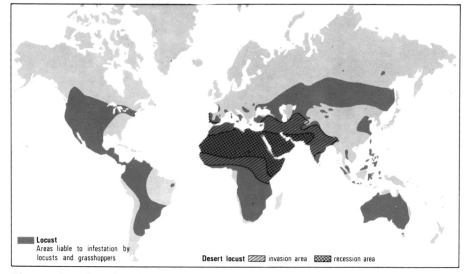

The map above shows the wide distribution of locusts. In some places, like North America, cultivation of their breeding grounds has reduced their numbers. In Africa, however, the desert locust is public enemy number one. Other locusts are easier to control, because after their migrations they recede to small areas; the desert locusts' outbreak area is very wide, as indicated.

Locust

Although the term 'locust' is loosely applied to any large tropical or subtropical grasshopper, it is better restricted to those whose numbers occasionally build up to form enormous migrating swarms which may do catastrophic damage to vegetation, notably cultivated crops and plantations.

Africa suffers most seriously from locust swarms and three species are of special importance. These are the desert locust, the red-legged locust and the African subspecies of the migratory locust.

Both the red locust and the African migratory locust have their own regional control organisations which effectively prevent plague outbreaks. The desert locust, however, presents a real international problem which has yet to be solved and is the main subject of study of the Anti-Locust Research Centre in London. It will therefore be the main subject of this entry.

△ *At the beginning of the rainy season the locust swarms mature, turn yellow and mate. In this picture a mature yellow male is mating with a precocious pink female which may thus be speeded to maturation.*

◁ *Immature pink adult female. Millions of these exist in vast swarms, which follow the wind to arrive in new breeding grounds soon after rain. Most damage is done in this migratory period: crops are eaten entirely and trees broken by the weight of settling locusts.*

◁ *Closeup of a yellow and black hopper. While the hoppers are marching they have a daily routine, based on temperature; at sunrise they descend from their roosts in low vegetation and warm up in the sun. Once their bodies are at a working temperature they march until the ground heat of midday forces them to climb into another roost, and resume the journey in the afternoon. While 'snack bar' feeding occurs en route, the main meal is taken in the early evening.*

▽▽▷ *Menace to come: hopper bands on the march, eating all the way. When they set out, they move only a few yards a day, but they hop for up to a mile in the later stages.*

◁ *About 4 in. beneath the soil the chain of locust life starts as a female pushes her abdomen into the moist layer to lay her eggs. Pending suitable conditions she can postpone maturation for 3 weeks but once ripe must lay in 3 days, and if sandy, moist soil beneath a dry coating cannot be found she will leave eggs anywhere, and they will die. Flooding or drought, too, help restrict locusts before birth.*

Shell Photograph

Shell Photograph

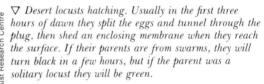

◁ *Pod of 70—80 locust eggs. When laying the female secretes a quick-drying froth around them and fills the hole with it, forming a pod with a porous plug at the top. The end of the plug is just below the surface, preventing sand falling into the hole and ensuring an easy exit for the hatchlings.*

Anti Locust Research Centre

▽ *Desert locusts hatching. Usually in the first three hours of dawn they split the eggs and tunnel through the plug, then shed an enclosing membrane when they reach the surface. If their parents are from swarms, they will turn black in a few hours, but if the parent was a solitary locust they will be green.*

Stephen Dalton NHPA

Shell Photograph

◁ *Trio of swarming hoppers. These come together to form dense groups, which join others to become a massive band. At this stage they are particularly vulnerable; ants carry them off, fly parasites infect them and birds take advantage of the feast they present.*

JB Free

Locust or gregarious grasshopper

The vast plagues of locusts which periodically create such havoc in many regions of the underdeveloped world are really nothing more nor less than hordes of gregarious grasshoppers. For locusts can exist in two phases: a solitary, grasshopper phase, or a swarming locust phase. When the grasshoppers are crowded together they change their behaviour, and, if kept like this for a generation or more, also change their shape and colour to that of the swarming form.

Solitary locusts come together only for mating and then behave very much as other grasshoppers do. The eggs, the size of rice grains, are laid down to 4 in. below the surface of the ground. They are held together by a frothy secretion which hardens to form an egg-pod $1\frac{1}{2}-2$ in. long, which usually contains 80—100 eggs. Above the pod the froth forms a plug which helps prevent the eggs from drying out and stops sand falling into the hole, so the hatchlings can escape. The egg stage lasts about 10—14 days in the main summer breeding areas but may be up to 70 days in the colder North African spring. The insects that hatch grow through a series of moults or skin-changes in the course of which they become gradually more like adult locusts and in the final 2 moults the wings form, becoming functional after the last moult, when the insect is adult. This takes 30—50 days, mainly depending on temperature. In a swarm the adults are pink at first, but after a few weeks or months, usually coinciding with the rainy seasons, they mature sexually and become yellow. The flightless immature locusts are traditionally known as 'hoppers'.

When they first hatch young solitary locusts disperse and unless some environmental factor forces them together they never do begin to associate in bands but settle down to the solitary life of grasshoppers. These are usually green or brown, blending well with their surroundings.

Jekyll and Hyde phase-change

Under certain conditions, depending on many variable factors, often associated with the weather, scattered solitary locusts may become concentrated into favourable laying sites. With every female locust laying two or three batches of 70—80 eggs each the numbers after hatching will have multiplied at least 100 times. With many more hoppers crowded into the same area, groups coalesce and they are then well on the way to the all important phase change from solitary to gregarious type which leads eventually to hopper bands and locust swarms.

When crowded together their colour changes to a bold pattern of black and orange or yellow stripes which probably helps them see one another and so keep together. The brightly patterned, crowded hoppers grow into pink adults which turn yellow at sexual maturity, solitary adults being sandy-coloured. Moreover, in the adults there are structural differences between the solitary and gregarious phases, notably in the wing, which is relatively longer in the gregarious phase. It is known that structural changes between one phase and another are associated with relative differences in the insects' hormonal balance.

Mutual stimulation leads to greater activity and they start to 'march'. Because an urge to keep close together is induced by development in the gregarious phase they march together in bands.

As adults they continue to migrate, and the urge to crowd together is maintained, but they are now airborne and move much faster. Weather conditions too can lead to the development of gregarious locusts and swarm formations. Scattered flying locusts fly downwind towards frontal systems of converging airflow and thus tend to accumulate in rainy areas. As the region inhabited by the desert locust is mainly arid, the result of persistently flying with the wind is to concentrate large numbers of locusts in areas when rain is likely to fall and provide them with food in the form of a flush of desert plants springing up after the rain. The gregarious phase develops in the offspring and migration then takes place in the usual way, following the prevailing wind and the favourable weather.

Locust plagues

When the swarm descends the locusts devour everything green. After mating takes place each female lays several hundred eggs. The young that hatch are still crowded and behave in just the same way, but the swarm that results can be many times larger. This swarm continues to migrate and again descends and multiplies its numbers. In this way a swarm may cover vast areas and build itself up into an aggregate of thousands of tons of locusts resulting in plague conditions. Plagues eventually come to an end due to adverse weather. The few survivors revert to the solitary phase, in which they are relatively harmless.

Perhaps the most important discovery made by the Anti-Locust Research Organisation has been that the African migratory locust and the red locust change from the solitary to the gregarious phase only in certain limited outbreak areas. These areas are effectively policed by regional locust control organisations and plague outbreaks have been prevented since 1944.

The desert locust is the locust of the Bible, and now by far the most damaging of all. It is hard to control because it has no geographically determined outbreak areas. It ranges over a vast area, from southern Spain and Asia Minor, the whole of northern Africa, through Iran to Bangladesh and India, an area comprising about 60 countries. Between plagues lasting 6 or more years there are equally long recessions when only solitary locusts are to be found. The last plague ran from 1950 to 1962 and another showed all the signs of building up rapidly after the spring rains of 1967. In 1968 the situation looked very serious but by mid-1969 it was much quieter than expected 6 months previously. The last outbreak was in 1973-4 in New South Wales, Queensland and Victoria.

Natural enemies

If all the locusts in a swarm only 2 miles square were to breed successfully, in only four generations there would be a severe infestation of the whole 196 million square miles of the earth's surface. Fortunately there is enormous mortality from natural causes. Winds may fail to carry the locusts

to a suitable breeding area. The soil may not be moist enough for the eggs to hatch. Or they hatch to find insufficient plant growth for their food or to protect them from the heat of the midday sun. There are also many predators, parasites and diseases of locusts. A little fly *Stomorhina* lays its eggs on top of the locust egg pods as soon as they are laid and the fly's grubs eat up the eggs. Larvae of the beetle *Trox* can destroy an egg field completely and ants have been seen waiting at the top of an egg froth plug and carrying away all the hatchlings. Flocks of birds often accompany both hopper bands and adult swarms and they can account for enormous numbers of hoppers; 1 448 hoppers were counted in the gut of a single stork.

Control by man

Concentrated insecticides and highly efficient spray gear using both aircraft and ground vehicles are used in enormous campaigns against desert locusts. One of the most effective, because it is simple and cheap, uses the exhaust gases from a Land Rover to produce a fine spray of poison. This will drift over the vegetation in the path of hoppers and is a very quick and economical way of killing hopper bands. Aircraft can match the mobility of a migrating swarm; searching greater areas, finding and following swarms (which are easier to see from the air) and spraying them in the morning and evening when they fly low and are most vulnerable to spraying. A single light aircraft carrying 60 gallons of insecticide can destroy 180 million locusts.

Migrating swarms of locusts commonly travel between 1 000 and 3 000 miles between successive breeding areas and naturally cross many international frontiers. Regional locust control organisations within the desert locust invasion areas pool resources and facilitate the movement of supplies across frontiers. These organisations in turn are coordinated by the Food and Agriculture Organisation (FAO) of the United Nations with its headquarters in Rome. FAO cooperates with the Desert Locust Information Service run by the Anti-Locust Research Centre in London.

phylum	**Arthropoda**
class	**Insecta**
order	**Orthoptera**
family	**Acrididae**
genera & species	***Austroicestes cruciata*** *Australian plague grasshopper* ***Chortoicetes terminifera*** *Australian plague locust* ***Locusta migratoria manilensis*** *Oriental migratory locust* ***Locusta migratoria migratoria*** *Asiatic migratory locust* ***Locusta migratoria migratorioides*** *African migratory locust* ***Melanoplus spretus*** *Rocky Mountain locust* ***Nomadacris septemfasciata*** *red locust* ***Schistocerca gregaria*** *desert locust*

Loggerhead

The loggerhead turtle is one of the sea turtles, distinguished from the green turtle (p. 1096) by its larger head and by the arrangement of the plates on the shell which is olive or reddish brown above and yellowish underneath. The shell is longer than it is broad, reaching 40 in. length, but is not usually more than 3 ft broad. The weight of a loggerhead is usually not more than 300 lb, but before their numbers were reduced individuals of 900 lb were known. Young loggerheads have three keels running down the

turtle eats seaweed. The loggerhead is, in fact, omnivorous, eating seaweed as well as fish, floating crustaceans, molluscs and jelly-fish. Like the hawksbill turtle, the logger-head eats the very poisonous Portuguese man-o'-war, attacking with its eyes closed. It would seem, however, that more protection than this is needed as the nemato-cysts or stinging cells of these animals can penetrate rubber gloves and the hard skeleton of a crab. Even if the leathery skin of the turtle is proof against the nematocysts the delicate membranes of the alimentary canal would not be, so we must assume that turtles are immune to the poison of Portuguese men-o'-war, and of the other jellyfish they eat with relish.

assisted with a strain and a grunt by the turtle. The clutch averages around 120, the maximum being 140. On completing the clutch the pit is filled in with sand, by a process similar to that of excavation except that sand is shovelled in, not out. First the egg pit is filled in, then the body pit. The foreflippers push sand backwards and the hindflippers rake it in. Every now and then the turtle moves forward pushing a heap of sand behind it, so filling in the hole and lifting itself out. Sand is scattered widely so that a large area appears churned and the actual nest is difficult to find.

The eggs hatch in 8–10 weeks, the baby turtles digging themselves out of the sand together and rushing down the beach.

△ *Appearances are deceptive. Loggerheads can be very aggressive.*

△ *Hand signals from a submarine traveller. Loggerhead turtle turning.*

carapace but these disappear as they get older until only the middle one is left. The range of the loggerhead extends farther into temperate waters than other turtles. It is the only turtle to breed on the coasts of the mainland of the United States. Once the loggerhead bred as far north as Virginia on the east coast. It still breeds in Florida and Georgia and California on the west coast. To the south, it is found near the River Plate in northern Argentina. The loggerhead also breeds on the coasts of Africa, Asia and Australia. Another unusual feature of the loggerhead's distribution is that it occasionally wanders up rivers. One was found in Loch Lomond, Scotland, and another in the Illinois River, a tributary several hundred miles up the Mississippi River.

Distasteful turtle

The eggs of loggerheads are eagerly sought after and at one time could be bought in the markets of Savannah and Charleston, but the flesh has never been popular. It is said to be tough and stringy and that the reason for this is that the loggerhead is a flesh-eater, whereas the more tender green

The strain of egg-laying

On the eastern seaboard of the United States loggerheads breed between April and August, and in Natal, South Africa, the breeding season runs from November to January. Unlike leathery turtles which seem to prefer open beaches that they can approach without having to manoeuvre and where they will not be in danger of tearing their soft skin, loggerheads nest on beaches guarded by rocks and reefs, where they feed before coming ashore. Logger-heads crawl about 300 ft up the shore, farther than the leathery turtles when they nest on the same beaches. Otherwise their nesting habits are very similar.

The first stage in nesting is to dig the body pit, throwing sand sideways until the turtle is lying in a hole about 6 in. deep. This takes about 15–30 minutes. Then, after a short rest, the egg pit is excavated, lifting out cupfuls of sand with the hindflippers until it is 8 in. deep. While crawling up the beach turtles are very easily disturbed and will retreat into the waves, but once they have started to dig they continue until the job is done and the turtle's movements can be watched by torchlight. On two occasions some scientists studying turtles helped a turtle with mutilated flippers dig her nest.

Egg-laying takes 10–30 minutes. The eggs are dropped three or four at a time,

Truculent turtle

Loggerheads have a reputation for aggres-siveness and in Ceylon are called the 'dog turtles' because they try to bite their captors. They are not invariably aggressive but in 1905 the New York *Herald* published an account of a very vindictive loggerhead caught off Long Island. The turtle, weigh-ing 600 lb, had been caught alive but escaped. A $50 reward was offered and five men set out to look for it. They eventually found it asleep and attempted to harpoon it. A tremendous fight ensued as the turtle turned on the boat. The men beat it over the head with oars but the turtle bit each one in two. It also severely gashed one man's arm with a blow from a flipper. Eventually with the boat waterlogged, the turtle escaped. The men took 2 hours to paddle home with the stubs of their oars, vowing that they would never hunt another turtle, reward or no reward.

class	**Reptilia**
order	**Testudines**
family	**Chelonidae**
genus & species	*Caretta caretta*

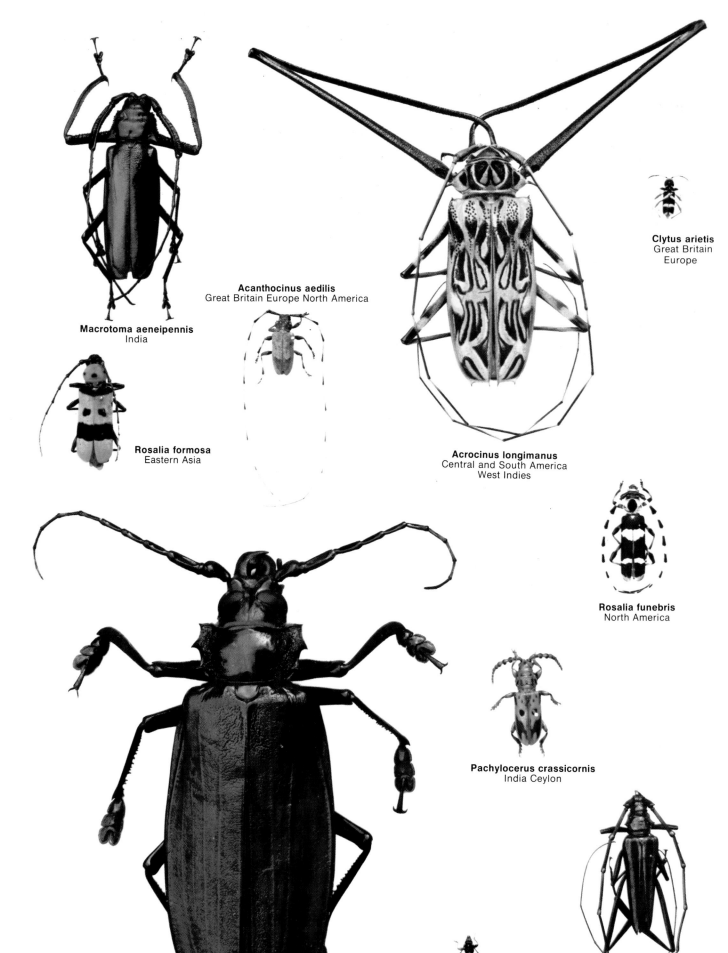

Macrotoma aeneipennis
India

Acanthocinus aedilis
Great Britain Europe North America

Rosalia formosa
Eastern Asia

Clytus arietis
Great Britain
Europe

Acrocinus longimanus
Central and South America
West Indies

Rosalia funebris
North America

Pachylocerus crassicornis
India Ceylon

Titanus giganteus
Amazons

Anubis mellyi
South Africa

Chloridolum klaessii
Southeast Asia

Longhorned beetle

The name used to describe the beetles of the family Cerambycidae, which number about 15 000 species, the great majority of which are tropical: only between 60 and 70 are British.

*The most obvious feature of longhorned beetles is the very long antennae, to which the name 'longhorn' or 'longicorn', as it is sometimes spelt, refers. An extreme form is seen in the genus **Acanthocinus** in which the antennae are four or more times the length of the body. When longhorned beetles settle they hold their antennae out like a pair of the large callipers used for measuring tree trunks. For this reason foresters call them 'timbermen'. Some of the tropical species are among the largest insects: **Xixuthrus heros** from Fiji is 6 in. long with its antennae as long again. The New World species of **Macrodontia** are equally large in the body but have rather short antennae and enormous spiky jaws, rather like those of a stag beetle.*

The longhorned beetles are of economic importance as pests of timber, as the larvae of many of them burrow in living or seasoned wood, making large tunnels which weaken it and spoil it for structural purposes.

Among the British species are the spotted longhorn, often seen on flowers in summer, and the two-banded longhorn. The musk beetle lives in old willows and is noted for its pleasant scent. It is now far less common than formerly.

Creaking beetles
Adult longhorn beetles are usually found on or near the trees in which the larvae feed, often hiding under loose bark. They also visit wild flowers on which they sun themselves and feed on the pollen. Many of them fly well, and they may be attracted to lights at night. Some of the large tropical species bite quite effectively if handled, and there are also species which make a creaking noise (stridulation) which is doubtless a defence reaction. This may be done either by moving the thorax up and down, producing friction between it and the abdomen or by scraping the hindlegs against the edges of the wing-cases.

Exceptional wood-eaters
The larvae of most longhorn beetles feed inside the stems of plants and often inside trees, either under the bark or burrowing in the solid wood. Most species are attached to one or a few kinds of tree; in Britain poplar, willow and oak suffer most from the attention of longhorns. The eggs are laid on the bark and the tiny larvae burrow in. As they grow they develop into large white or yellowish grubs with round instead of the usual flattened heads and extremely powerful jaws with which they can rasp away the hardest heartwoods. Most insects which feed on wood cannot directly digest the cellulose: either they must devour great quantities of wood, like the caterpillar of the goat moth to get the non-cellulose protein, or they have bacteria or protozoans in the alimentary canal which break down the cellulose as in termites and stag-beetles. The grubs of longhorned beetles are exceptional in having a digestive enzyme that breaks down cellulose.

Most of the larvae take 2−3 years to reach full size and some take a good deal longer. When nearly ready to change into the pupa the larva makes a tunnel to the exterior and then stops it up with a plug of wood fibres or a cap of hardened chalky mucus. When the beetle emerges from the pupa it pushes or bites its way out. The adult beetle is quite unable to gnaw its way through solid wood but it can bite through the plug made by the larva.

The grubs that live in the heartwood are fairly safe from enemies, but those that live under bark or in decayed wood are favourite prey of woodpeckers. There is a large longhorn beetle found in New Zealand whose grubs, known by the name of 'hu-hu', are regarded as a delicacy by the Maoris.

Camouflage and mimicry
The longhorned beetles are extremely varied in colour and marking, and some of them show adaptive coloration in great perfection. The big African species *Pterognatha gigas* lies along a twig with its antennae extended in front and is coloured and mottled to look exactly like a patch of moss. Perhaps more remarkable are the numerous cases of longhorned beetles which have come to resemble other insects that are distasteful or poisonous, and so are left alone by predators. Many examples of mimicry of this kind are known from the tropics, and there is one quite common British species, the wasp beetle, whose black and yellow stripes give it a strong resemblance to a wasp. Its antennae are abnormally short for a beetle of this family; they are in fact hardly longer than a wasp's antennae!

An insect Methuselah
The larvae of the house longhorn live in dry, seasoned softwoods and are a pest of structural timber in Europe and some parts of England, especially northwestern Surrey. where a large percentage of buildings are infested. The beetle is greyish-black with two lighter grey marks across the wing-cases. It is covered with hair except for two areas on the thorax, which are bare and shining and look like eyes. The larva grows to an inch in length, and in warm weather the rasping of its jaws, as it feeds, is distinctly audible. Its dry and austere diet makes it very slow-growing, and it seldom reaches full size in less than 3 years and not uncommonly lives for ten. One case is known of a larva that lived for 32 years before the beetle emerged from the wood; this is probably the longest life span known for any insect.

phylum	**Arthropoda**
class	**Insecta**
order	**Coleoptera**
family	**Cerambycidae**
genera & species	***Aromia moschata*** *musk beetle* ***Clytus arietis*** *wasp beetle* ***Hylotrupes bajulus*** *house longhorn* ***Rhagium bifasciatum*** *2-banded longhorn* ***Strangalia maculata*** *spotted longhorn* *others*

◁ *Museum specimens show the extensive size and colour range of longhorned beetles (natural size).*

▽ ***Geloharpya confluens*** *attacked by ants from the lowveld of South Africa (⅔ natural size).*

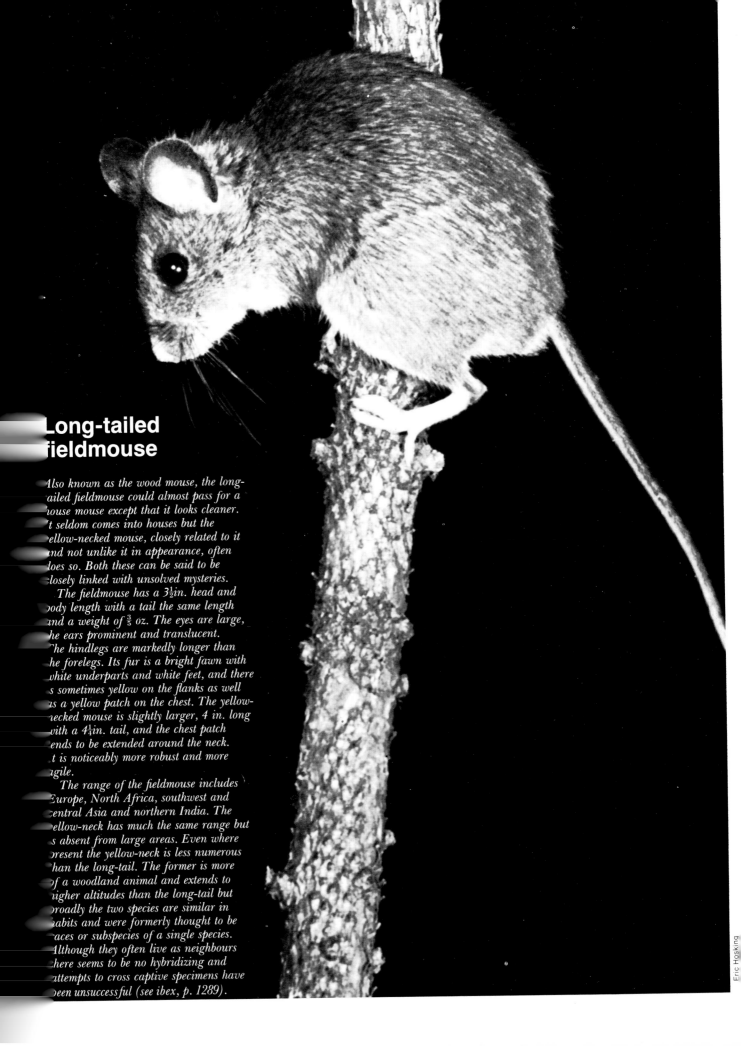

Long-tailed fieldmouse

Also known as the wood mouse, the long-tailed fieldmouse could almost pass for a house mouse except that it looks cleaner. It seldom comes into houses but the yellow-necked mouse, closely related to it and not unlike it in appearance, often does so. Both these can be said to be closely linked with unsolved mysteries.

The fieldmouse has a 3½in. head and body length with a tail the same length and a weight of ⅗ oz. The eyes are large, the ears prominent and translucent. The hindlegs are markedly longer than the forelegs. Its fur is a bright fawn with white underparts and white feet, and there is sometimes yellow on the flanks as well as a yellow patch on the chest. The yellow-necked mouse is slightly larger, 4 in. long with a 4¼in. tail, and the chest patch tends to be extended around the neck. It is noticeably more robust and more agile.

The range of the fieldmouse includes Europe, North Africa, southwest and central Asia and northern India. The yellow-neck has much the same range but is absent from large areas. Even where present the yellow-neck is less numerous than the long-tail. The former is more of a woodland animal and extends to higher altitudes than the long-tail but broadly the two species are similar in habits and were formerly thought to be races or subspecies of a single species. Although they often live as neighbours there seems to be no hybridizing and attempts to cross captive specimens have been unsuccessful (see ibex, p. 1289).

Midnight cairn-builders

The long-tailed fieldmouse lives in woods, fields, hedgerows and gardens, making runways under leaf litter and extensive tunnel systems underground with entrance holes of about 1½ in. diameter. It is more active at night but can sometimes be seen by day. It tends to live in clans based on a hierarchy with a dominant male, and when brushwood that has covered the ground for some time is removed numbers of long-tails will be uncovered. Nests, usually underground, are made of finely shredded grass and used for sleeping, as well as breeding, and disused birds' nests, even at a fair height in trees, may be used for these purposes as well as for storing food. Each family has a home range of ¼ acre or more and long-tails tested have homed for certain from ¼ mile, half of them from nearly ½ mile.

Occasionally small cairns of stones about 2 in. high and the same across are found immediately beside or even over the entrance to a burrow without blocking it. The purpose is unknown. After a while the cairn will be dismantled and the stones scattered over an area of several square yards. Conversely, if someone scatters them the identical pebbles will be retrieved and rebuilt over or beside the same entrance.

Long-tails often bound, kangaroo-fashion, but unlike kangaroos they bring all four feet to the ground for each leap, and each leap may be up to 4 ft long.

Food hoarding

The main food is seeds, grain, acorns, nuts, fruit, buds, seedlings, fungi, insects and snails. Hazel nuts are gnawed open leaving an irregular hole at the blunt end. Snail shells are gnawed through. Males eat more insects and less green food than females, juveniles eat more buds and fungi and fewer insects. A feature of both long-tails and yellow-necks is hoarding. This seems to take place whenever a crop is available, whether acorns, hazel nuts, holly berries; a pint to a quart of nuts or berries being commonplace in such caches. Where the contents are nuts it is usual for people finding them to say squirrels have done it. In fact, the squirrels living in the same area as the two mice bury nuts and acorns singly, rarely if ever in a hoard. If such a hoard is taken and scattered over an area of ¼ acre all will be collected and re-hoarded in a few hours and in broad daylight.

In step with mother

Breeding begins in March and continues until October, and right through the winter if it is mild. There is a peak of breeding in July – August. Gestation is 25 – 26 days. Each female may have 5 litters a year of up to 6 in each litter. The young, born blind, first leave the nest at 16 days and are weaned at 21 days. They are said to start breeding at the age of 5 months. When they first make excursions from the nest the young may be seen running behind the mother holding on to her teats. She may be carrying one in the mouth and 2 or 3 hanging on. The mother seems not to be inconvenienced nor slowed down by this.

Multiple enemies

Several mammals and birds eat long-tails and yellow-necks. Owls, and tawny owls especially, weasels, stoats, foxes and other small or medium carnivores are the main predators, but even the carrion crow will kill young ones.

Quiet as a mouse

Yellow-necks come into houses in autumn and depart into the open at the end of winter. In old houses, with cavity walls and plenty of space under the floorboards, they will bring in quantities of nuts from distances of up to 100 yards and transport them up the walls to the top story of the house. In the quiet of the night a yellow-neck bounding along under the floorboards makes a good imitation of a person walking across the room with a heavy tread. In two houses at least in southern England, with reputations of being haunted, it can be said beyond reasonable doubt that the ghostly visitations were only yellow-necked mice.

The second mystery caused a stir in South Devon in February 1855. After an overnight fall of snow, hoofprints were seen going over the ground, under bushes, over rooftops and haystacks and along the tops of walls. In one place the tracks went up to a wall and started again the other side, as if something had walked straight through the wall. The tracks went here and there to a total of some 100 miles. Many people have tried to solve the mystery of this strange visitation that made Devon people lock their doors at night in the weeks that followed. Some explanations have been fantastic, others prosaic, but the story has come down to us as the night of the devil's hoofprints. In 1964, Alfred G Leutscher, eminent British naturalist, took photographs of the footprints in snow of bounding long-tails. They showed U-shaped prints 1½×1 in., at 8 in. intervals – the dimensions recorded for the devil's hoofprints seen in Devon.

class	**Mammalia**
order	**Rodentia**
family	**Muridae**
genus & species	*Apodemus sylvaticus* long-tailed fieldmouse *A. flavicollis* yellow-necked mouse

△ *Devil's footprints? No, only those of a wood mouse whose bounding tracks in the snow look like cloven hoof marks.*
◁ *Splitting hairs. Long-tailed fieldmouse meticulously combs out any dirt from his fur.*

Jane Burton: Photo Res

Jane Burton: Photo Res

1473

Lorikeet

Lorikeets are colourful little parrots. They are predominantly green, usually an olive green, with small beaks and short to moderately long tails, and they range in size from 6—15 in. All have patches of other colours, reds, blues and yellows, sometimes purple, brown and black, in patches on the head, neck and breast.

The little lorikeet, $6\frac{1}{2}$ in. long, is greenish, with a brilliant crimson face. The purple-crowned lorikeet, also $6\frac{1}{2}$ in. long, has a purple crown, patches of red and yellow on the head and a pale blue throat and breast changing behind to yellow. The rainbow lorikeet, 11 in. long, just fails to have in its plumage literally all the colours in the rainbow. Its back, wings and the upperside of the tail are the usual green but elsewhere the plumage is most variegated and is set off by a bright red beak. The rainbow lorikeet is divided into 21 subspecies which range over the islands of the East Indies and Polynesia as well as over eastern Australia. The scaly-breasted lorikeet of Australia— so named because its breast feathers look like overlapping scales—has little variation from the typical greenish colour, apart from its red beak, until it raises its wings showing the red and yellow underside margined with the dark brown of the flight feathers. Lorikeets as a group are distributed over the Malay Archipelago, Polynesia and Australia.

Together with the lories, the lorikeets or honey-parrots make up the subfamily Loriinae of the parrot family. There are 31 species some of which are divided into subspecies, making 73 different kinds of lorikeets each with its common name.

Indescribable colours

Lorikeets are swift in flight and usually move about in flocks. They are to a large extent nomadic, following the seasonal blossoming of the eucalyptus and other flowering trees. As they climb about the trees they keep up a high-pitched chattering and screeching, but if the effect on the ear is not especially pleasant, the combination of bright blossoms with brilliant birds intermingling is wonderful to the eye. John Gould, famous for his studies of Australian animals, wrote: 'I scarcely believe that it is possible to convey an idea of the appearance of a forest of flowering gums tenanted by *Trichoglossi* (lorikeets); three or four species being frequently seen on the same tree and often simultaneously attacking pendant blossoms of the same branch.' As suddenly as a flock descends on a tree so it will suddenly take flight again, still chattering, their combined wings adding a loud rushing sound. Alec H Chisholm, Australian ornithologist, has given us a modern version of Gould's words: 'It is difficult to imagine the Australian landscape lacking these happy honey-lovers that go shouting and screeching from district to district throughout the year, following the flow of gum-blossoms.'

High society—rainbow and scaly-breasted lorikeets survey the world from their treetop perch.

Lorikeets take little notice of people. On the contrary, they seem especially tame and this led to the Griffiths sanctuary at Currumbin, Queensland, where rainbow and scaly-breasted lorikeets came by the score each day to be fed by hand. In due course the sanctuary became a visiting place where people could enjoy the spectacle while the lorikeets perched freely on their heads and hands. Other people have attracted lorikeets similarly by putting out sugar water.

Hard on the blossoms

These beautiful birds feed mainly on nectar and they probably play a major part in the pollination of the trees they visit. Other nectar-eating birds have thin tubular bills for siphoning the sweet liquids. Lorikeets crush the blossoms with their beaks and lap up the juices with their tongues as well as inserting the tongue skilfully into the flowers to lap up nectar with its brush tip. They also eat buds and fruit, and flocks of lorikeets visiting orchards can be a pest. Apart from other damage the ground beneath a tree may be littered with fallen blossoms broken off by the lorikeets in their eagerness to get at the nectar.

Bright youngsters

The nest is without soft lining materials in a hole in a tree trunk or in the cavity at the end of a broken branch, fairly high above ground. The breeding season is from May to December or January, 2—4 white eggs being laid and incubated by the hen only for three weeks to a month. The chicks soon become covered with a grey down and leave the nest fully fledged 9—10 weeks after hatching. Although the hen does the incubating her mate is in fairly close attendance and accompanies her when she leaves the nest and he escorts her back.

While in the nest the baby lorikeets are in semi-darkness and they have what appear to be luminous edges to the beak, which act as a guide to the parent putting food down their throats. The story is told of a man who climbed 50 ft to the nest of a scaly-breasted lorikeet. On looking into the cavity in the tree he saw two bright objects, luminous and resembling eyes, that moved in the darkness. Suspecting these were the eyes of a snake he lit a magnesium flare and from its light saw two baby lorikeets.

The enemies of lorikeets are the birds of prey. A flock of them passing overhead can be sent diving for cover when somebody makes the call of an Australian goshawk.

Space saving

There are all kinds of reasons for particular scientific names. An animal may be named after the person who first found it or after the place where it was found. The name may, on the other hand, indicate the outstanding feature of the animal. Sometimes a name is misspelt when first it appears in print and by the strict 'law of priority' this name should stand even if it offends the purists. The oddest one of all is the name of the rainbow lorikeet *Trichoglossus haematod*. Most people spell it *haemotodus*, which is what it should be from an etymological point of view. When it was first used, however, the name came at the end of a line and the last syllable was left out to avoid overrunning the name onto the next line.

class	**Aves**
order	**Psittaciformes**
family	**Psittacidae**
genera & species	***Glossopsitta pusilla*** *little lorikeet* ***G. porphyrocephala*** *purple-crowned lorikeet* ***Trichoglossus chlorolepidotus*** *scaly-breasted lorikeet* ***T. haematodus*** *rainbow lorikeet*

Loris

Lorises are slow-moving lemuroids of Asia, closely related to the African potto and angwantibo (p. 135). They have broad, grasping hands and feet. The hand has an enlarged thumb and much reduced index finger, though not as much as in their African relatives. In each forearm and shank is a network of blood vessels called the **rete mirabile,** which slows down blood flow and allows the animal to clamp onto a branch for long periods at a time. Lorises, being nocturnal, have big eyes. Like all the lemurs they have a claw on the second toe and comb-like front teeth, both used in grooming.

There are three species of loris. The slender loris of southern India and Ceylon is 10–15 in. long, grey-brown with black eye-rings. It has a pointed muzzle and slender limbs; the forelimbs are almost stick-like. The slow loris is much plumper, and the limbs are shorter and stouter. Its muzzle is rounded, its colour more brown than grey with a brown or black back stripe which forks on the crown, sending a branch to each ear and eye, joining with the eye-rings. The fore-part of the back, especially surrounding the dorsal stripe, tends to have long frosted tips to the hairs, making it look ashy or silvery white. The lesser slow loris has less woolly hair and is only 8–10 in. long. The slow loris is found from Bengal and Indo-China to Java and Borneo, the lesser slow loris is restricted to Vietnam, where it is found in the same forests as the larger species, without interbreeding.

In 1960 Professor Dao Van Tien described a third species of slow loris as **Nycticebus intermedius,** being supposedly halfway between the slow and the lesser slow loris in size. Further study of the lesser slow loris has, however, shown that it is larger than had previously been thought, and that it was originally described on a young specimen, so **Nycticebus intermedius** is, in fact, just the adult of the lesser slow loris. These same studies showed that the two loris genera are not as different as formerly supposed, and in many of its skull and teeth characters the lesser slow loris partially bridges the gap. It is small, like the slender loris, with a long snout, and partially obliterated markings; but it is still plump and a real 'slow' loris—not at all 'slender'.

Day sleepers

The painstaking hand over hand movements of the lorises have a purpose. It has been suggested that these help them to creep up unobserved on their prey, such as a nesting bird, with a final swoop at the end with the hands grabbing the prey quickly. They feed on fruit and leaves, also insects, birds, small mammals and reptiles. The slender loris is found in tropical rain forest, swamp forest or dry woodland; the slow lorises are restricted to tropical rain forest. All are solitary, sleeping by day rolled up into a ball and coming out at night. While asleep they grasp a branch with all four feet and tuck their head between them.

In captivity, the slender loris generally remains rather bad-tempered. The slow loris is also bad-tempered at first, but more

▽ *Baby love – the young slender loris clings tenderly to its mother's back.*

△ *Sense of security – the same wide-eyed youngster slung under its mother's belly.*

▽ *Plump slow loris showing the brown stripe down its back to full advantage.*

often becomes tame. When aroused, lorises growl and make a high-pitched chatter, and try to bite. Their firmness of grip is amazing and quite instinctive, being highly developed at birth. They sleep rolled into a ball with the hands and feet securely gripping the branch. Their movement is slow and deliberate, with only one foot being moved at a time while the others grasp the branch.

Clinging to mother

The slender loris is said to come into season twice a year, with a 5½ months interval between. The gestation is 6 months. In Ceylon these two sharply marked breeding seasons are April–May and November–December. The slow loris, living in a non-seasonal forest, has no such restricted breeding season. The female is in season every 42 days or so. Gestation is 90 days. The mother has one baby, sometimes two. It is born well-developed and clings to the mother's fur. Sometimes the mother places it on a branch where it clings tightly until she returns. Young stay with mother for a year.

Whistling the wind

These slow-moving, ghostly inhabitants of the forest, stealthily crawling along branches, are bound to be the source of a great many superstitions. Slender lorises are sold live in southern India for the sake of their eyes, which are sometimes believed to be love-charms. Tamil doctors use the eyes as a medicament for eye diseases. Similar tales surround slow lorises. Another belief arises from a single-note whistle slow lorises make at night. Nobody knows the purpose of this but as it is made with increased frequency by the female as she comes into season it may be a mating call. Chinese sailors used to take these animals to sea and listen for the whistle, which, they said, indicated the approach of a wind.

class	**Mammalia**	
order	**Primates**	
family	**Lorisidae**	
genera & species	***Loris tardigradus*** *slender loris*	
	Nycticebus coucang *slow loris*	
	N. pygmaeus *lesser slow loris*	

◁ *Page 1475: Dopey of Disney Land–with a sad expression and with extreme care the slender loris makes its slow way along a high branch.*
▽ *Holding on for dear life–this ball of curly fur, a young slender loris, is left stranded by its mother and waits longingly for her return.*

Lory

There are 52 kinds of parrots that are called lories: 25 species and 27 sub-species. They are closely related to the lorikeets, another group of parrots, but differ in being somewhat bigger and in having short tails, rounded or square at the end, instead of the long pointed tail of the lorikeet. The colour of lories is predominantly red, with yellow and green, instead of the green with yellow and red patches of lorikeets. The yellow-backed lory of the Moluccas is 10½ in. long and is a brilliant red with a splash of yellow on the back, green wings and a horn-coloured or orange bill. Its eyes are bright amber and its feet blackish-grey. The purple-capped or purple-naped lory, also of the Moluccas and other islands, is about the same size, and is a bright scarlet with green wings, blue shoulders and legs and the crown of the head blue-black. A broad yellow band tinged with red crosses the upper part of the breast and the tail feathers show a black band just behind the yellow tips. The bill is orange yellow. The predominance of red is shown in many common names of lories, such as cardinal lory and the various red lories, red and blue lories, carmine-fronted lory and red-quilled lory.

Lories live on the islands of the East Indies, notably on New Guinea, and on islands in the southwest Pacific.

◁ *Gilding the lily:* **Domicella garrula** *gives its paintbox plumage a fastidious once-over, leaving not a feather out of place.*

A taste for sweets

Lories are very like lorikeets in their habits (p. 1474). Both are brush-tongued, which means they have, instead of the usual thick, fleshy tongue of parrots, a slender tongue with a brush of long fleshy filaments, like thick hairs, at the tip. The beak is weak for a bird in the parrot family and the food is nectar and pollen as well as the pulp of fruits. Judging from some lories in captivity soft-bodied insects must sometimes be eaten. In one instance in which nestling lories were hand-fed, although they took mixtures of honey and various baby foods, including apple puree, when given mealworms they not only accepted these but showed a strong preference for them.

△ *A gymnastic investigation of events below.*
◁ *Perfectionist parrot: a lory cleans an awkward feather through its tight beak.*

Reared in secrecy

The yellow-backed lory has bred several times in aviaries. Two rounded white eggs are laid and incubated for about a month. In one case the male shared the incubation, in others it is not clear whether he did or not. In all cases the eggs were laid in a hollow log or an equivalent box, with peat or sawdust on the floor, with an opening so small that it was difficult to see what was going on inside. The nestlings first grow a covering of grey down, then in 3 weeks feathers begin to sprout and the eyes open. The parents feed them by regurgitation. By the time the young birds are partially feathered, at about one month, they have green wings, but without flight feathers and the yellow on the back. The red does not appear until later. The beak is black and so is the eye. Final fledging comes 2 months from hatching.

Photos by Cy Hwang

△ *Preening acrobatics — the lory cleans his wing feathers meticulously while holding on tightly to his swing.*

Rich merchant collectors

Although the number of kinds of lories known is large, our information on their habits is scanty, except such as can be gleaned from birds in captivity. Some of the species have long been favourite aviary birds, not only because of their colours but for their 'talking', the purple-capped lory being an example. The many other kinds are best known as skins in museum cabinets, and for these as well as collections of other bird skins we have to thank people like Maarten Dirk van Renesse van Duivenbode and his son Lodewijk. They were planters and merchants living in Ternate. They brought to the notice of ornithologists any strange birds passing through their hands, and several species are named after them. Alfred Russell Wallace met the father in 1858 and describes him as being of an ancient Dutch family, very rich, owning half the town, 'possessed many ships, and above a hundred slaves. He was, moreover, well educated and fond of literature and science — a phenomenon in these regions. He was generally known as the king of Ternate, from his large property and great influence with the native Rajahs and their subjects.' It was probably because of Wallace's visit that the van Duivenbodes sent out native hunters to neighbouring islands to collect bird skins.

class	**Aves**
order	**Psittaciformes**
family	**Psittacidae**
genera & species	*Chalcopsitta duivenbodei* Duivenbode's lory **Domicella domicella** purple-capped lory **D. garrula flavopalliata** yellow-backed lory, others

Lovebird

Lovebirds are small African parakeets named for their sociable habits. Pairs spend much of their time huddling together bill-to-bill. They mate for life and it has been said that a lovebird will die of grief if its mate dies. There is no proof of this, but many die of fright from sudden noises. Despite this, they are popular cage birds because of their brilliant plumage and 'loving' habits.

The six species of lovebird are all about 4 in. long, parrotlike in form and generally green in plumage. The back and wings are usually darker green than the underparts and several species have a grey rump. The Abyssinian, red-faced, peach-faced, Nyasaland and Fischer's lovebirds have patches of red on the head, while the black-cheeked and masked lovebirds have black. The Madagascar lovebird has a white head and breast and Swindern's lovebird has a black collar. The black-cheeked, Nyasaland, masked and Fischer's lovebirds are races of a single species, Agapornis personata.

The closest relatives of the lovebirds are the hanging parakeets of Asia. The Madagascar, Abyssinian and red-faced lovebirds resemble these parakeets most closely. The sexes differ in plumage and a pair lives together, whereas in the other species there is no difference in plumage between the sexes and they nest in colonies. These lovebirds also share certain behavioural characteristics with the hanging parakeets described below.

Except for the Madagascar lovebirds, all lovebirds live on the mainland of Africa south of the Sahara. The red-faced and Swindern's lovebirds are found in many parts of equatorial Africa and the peach-faced lovebird is found in southwest Africa. The Nyasaland and black-cheeked lovebirds have restricted ranges, limited to stretches of the Zambesi River.

Sleeping straphangers

The hanging parakeets are also known as bat parakeets and both names refer to their habit of roosting upside down. They hang from the branches of leafy trees in clusters and preen each other in this position after waking. The red-faced lovebird is the only one to behave in this extraordinary way, but the Madagascar lovebird bathes by hanging upside down in the rain with its wings and tail outspread.

Lovebirds eat a variety of food including seeds, fruit, nectar and insects. In places flocks of these parakeets do some damage to crops.

Wearing the nest

Another strange trait lovebirds share with hanging parakeets is that of carrying nest material in their feathers. All lovebirds prepare nest material by punching pieces out of leaves or tearing them into strips. The three species of lovebird most closely related to the hanging parakeets, together with the

*Lined up for inspection — a group of Fischer's lovebirds, **Agapornis personata fischeri***

Peter Hill

peach-faced lovebird, tuck the pieces of nest material into their feathers and carry them to their nest holes. The feathers are erected, half a dozen pieces of material are pushed in and the feathers are flattened to hold them in place. Each feather has minute hooks which stick it to its neighbours and hold the nest material in place. Even so, much of the cargo is lost, especially by the peach-faced lovebird, which carries long strips rather than small pieces. The lovebirds that carry small pieces of nest material build simple nests in holes dug in tree trunks or in the earthy nests that some ants make on branches. The others that carry leaves

and strips of bark in their bills build complicated nest chambers with entrance tunnels inside the nest holes.

At the start of courtship the male is wary of the female and alternately sidles towards her then retreats, twittering and bobbing his head. In some species he feeds her, while in others the female feeds the male. The eggs are incubated for 3 weeks and until the chicks fly, at 6 weeks old, they are fed by both parents. Towards the end of this period the male does most of the feeding.

The female of the lovebird species related closely to the hanging parakeets defends her nest against intruders. If disturbed she ruffles her feathers and partly spreads her wings and tail, appearing much larger, and at the same time she utters buzzing noises. Her chicks also ruffle their feathers and buzz. If the intruder does not retreat she suddenly flattens her plumage and lunges at the source of disturbance, giving every appearance of intending to bite but not in fact doing so. The lovebirds that nest in colonies do not show this behaviour but they mob any intruding predator, screaming at it and flapping their wings.

Muddled lovebirds

The lovebirds that carry nest material in their feathers are those that are most closely related to the hanging parakeets. They are the most primitive of the lovebirds. The more recently evolved species have reverted to the usual method of carrying nest material — in the bill. These species also build complicated nests in colonies and defend the nests by mobbing. These patterns of behaviour are instinctive, that is they are inherited, as experiments in crossbreeding lovebirds have shown. When peach-faced lovebirds, that carry material in the feathers, were mated with Fischer's lovebirds, a subspecies of masked lovebird that carries material in its bill, the offspring had great difficulty in carrying any material at all. At first they were completely confused. They could cut up nest material competently but did not know how to carry it. They picked it up, tried to tuck it into the feathers but could not hold it there. After playing about for some time they sometimes managed to carry some material in their bills. This suggested that the unfortunate lovebirds had inherited the patterns of nesting behaviour from both parents. Instincts are, however, capable of modification by learning and after 3 years the hybrid lovebirds had learnt to carry nest material in their bills, and could also tuck it into their feathers quite efficiently.

class	**Aves**		
order	**Psittaciformes**		
family	**Psittacidae**		
genus & species	***Agapornis cana*** *Madagascar lovebird* **A. personata** *masked lovebird* **A. pullaria** *red-faced lovebird* **A. roseicollis** *peach-faced lovebird* **A. swinderniana** *Swindern's lovebird* **A. taranta** *Abyssinian lovebird*		

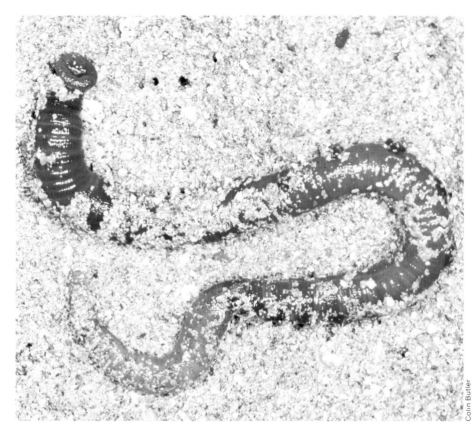

Colin Butler

About to burrow — the European lugworm with its swollen oval proboscis everted and ready to start digging a new U-shaped home in the sand for its rhythmic existence.

Lugworm

This is a large worm living in sand on the seabed. Its coiled castings are a familiar sight on a beach at low tide but the animal itself is not seen except by those who, from curiosity or to use it as fish bait, dig the worm out of the sand.

Fully grown, the lugworm of the coasts of Europe is up to 9 in. long and $\frac{3}{8}$ in. diameter. Other species on the North American coasts range from 3 to 12 in. The body is, like that of an earthworm, ringed or segmented. Its head end, which is blackish red and bears no tentacles or bristles, passes into a fatter middle part which is red. This in turn passes into a thinner yellowish red tail end. The middle part has bristles along its sides and also pairs of feathery gills. There is a well developed system of bloodvessels with red blood rich in the oxygen-carrying pigment, haemoglobin.

Life in a burrow
A lugworm lives in a U-shaped burrow in sand. The U is made up of an L-shaped gallery lined with mucus, from the toe of which a vertical unlined shaft runs up to the surface. This is the head shaft. At the surface the head shaft is marked by a small saucer-shaped depression. The tail shaft, 2–3 in. from it, is marked by a much coiled casting of sand. The lugworm lies in this burrow with its head at the base of the head shaft, swallowing sand from time to time. This makes the column of sand drop slightly, so there is a periodic sinking of the sand in

the saucer-shaped depression. When it first digs its burrow the lugworm softens the sand in the head shaft by pushing its head up into it with a piston action. After that it is kept loose by a current of water driven through the burrow from the hind end by waves of contraction passing along the body.

Eating sand
The lugworm can move backwards and forwards in its burrow by waves of contraction and expansion of the body, using the bristles on the middle part of the body to grip the sides. It moves towards the head shaft to swallow sand and later moves backwards so its rear end goes up to the top of the tail shaft, in order to pass the indigestible sand out at the surface as a long thin cylinder. As the sand passes through the stomach and intestine small particles of dead plant and animal matter in it are digested. The sand is taken in by an evertible proboscis. That is, the front end of the throat can be pushed

out through the mouth as a swollen oval proboscis which gives out a sticky secretion to which sand and particles of food adhere. The proboscis is then pulled in again and the material sticking to it is swallowed. In one species the action of swallowing takes place every 5 seconds and after 8–15 swallows the lugworm rests for a few minutes. It takes about an hour for the sand to pass through the body. Then the lugworm moves backwards through the burrow and ejects this as the cylindrical castings familiar on the beach.

Burrowing babies
Once it has burrowed into the sand a lugworm seldom leaves it. It can stay there for weeks on end, sometimes changing its position in the sand. But it may leave the burrow completely and re-enter the sand, making a fresh burrow elsewhere. It does not leave the burrow for breeding but for two days in early October there is a genital crisis. This is when all the lugworms liberate their ova and sperms into the water above, and there the ova are fertilized. The ova are enclosed in tongue-shaped masses of jelly about 8 in. long, 3 in. wide and 1 in. thick. Each mass is anchored at one end. The larvae hatching from the eggs feed on the jelly and eventually break out when they have grown to a dozen segments and are beginning to look like their parents. They burrow into the sand, usually higher up the beach than the adults, and gradually move down the beach as they get older.

Safe underground
There is little information on the enemies of lugworms. We can be sure that they fall prey to bottom feeding animals at times and are sometimes eaten by seabirds probing the sand. They will be eaten mainly in the young stages when they are finding their first burrow or when seeking a new burrow as they move down the beach. Also their burrows will be nearer the surface and therefore more vulnerable. The burrows of adults are as much as 1 ft deep, sometimes twice this. Burrowing not only gives protection from living enemies but also from the elements, such as changes in temperature and violent wave action. The scour of the surface leaves them unharmed. Sand is disturbed to a depth of $\frac{2}{5}$ in. per 1 ft of wave-height, and it is seldom that the effect of waves is felt at more than 2 in. from the surface.

Underwater, head submerged in the sand the first stage of burrowing is in progress. The delicate red feathery tufts are the lugworm's paired gills which are well supplied with blood.

Heather Angel

1481

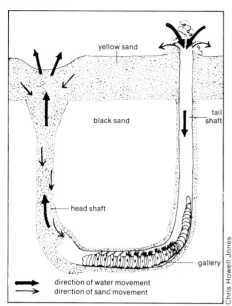

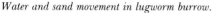

Water and sand movement in lugworm burrow.

Evening occupation when the tide is out—surrounded by lugworm casts two fishermen dig for bait.

Shift-working worm

Throughout each day a lugworm alternates bursts of activity with periods of rest. This pattern of behaviour is best described as being one of activity cycles. Each cycle is made up of several phases associated with feeding, irrigation of the burrow for breathing and defaecation. Irrigation follows feeding; the lugworm moves backwards in the burrow bringing its hind end near the exit to the tail shaft. The gut is emptied and then there follows a forward wave movement of the gills which draws water in through the tail shaft, along the burrow and past the head end, where it loosens the sand in the head shaft for the next bout of feeding. Next, the gills move tailwards, driving

the water once more over their surface. The irrigation movements take place about every 40 minutes. We can, therefore, visualize the lugworm in its tubular burrow swinging forward to feed and backward to defaecate and breathe, then swinging forward again, so driving water up into the sand in the head shaft and at the same time drawing water in from the tail shaft. It is a kind of pumping action that makes possible the functions of living.

The most important aspect of this cycle of activity is that the various movements in it arise spontaneously. A lugworm placed in a U-tube with only a small amount of water, and therefore a limited supply of oxygen, will continue its normal cycle. If the gullet is separated from the rest of the body it

will continue the movements that force the proboscis out to collect food. Just as a heart has its own pacemaker and continues to beat when removed from the body, so the various parts of the lugworm have their own pacemakers, the end result of which is to keep the animal moving backwards and forwards at regular intervals in its burrow to feed, get rid of waste and breathe.

phylum	**Annelida**
class	**Polychaeta**
family	**Arenicolidae**
genus & species	***Arenicola cristata*** N American ***A. marina*** European others

Lunar surface? No, just an unspoilt seaside landscape of saucer-shaped depressions and lugworm casts, the fisherman's paradise.

Cold-water carnivorous marine fish — young **Cyclopterus lumpus***, largest species of lumpsucker.*

The pelvic fins form an elaborate sucker.

Lumpsucker

There can hardly be another animal to exceed the lumpsucker fish in parental devotion. Even more surprisingly, the male gives us this remarkable instance of self-sacrifice.

The lumpsucker is stockily built, being up to 2 ft long and 13 lb weight. Its body is rounded and humped, ornamented with rows of tubercles. Its head is massive. The male is smaller than the female, a dark blue, almost black, with fins almost transparent and tinged with red, and he has a reddish belly, especially in the breeding season. The female is greenish with dark bluish patches, there is a reddish tinge on the pectoral fins and her belly is yellowish. On the underside of both is an elaborate and efficient sucker formed by the pelvic fins.

The largest species, which is also known as the sea-hen or henfish, from the tenacity with which the male sits guarding the eggs, is widely distributed in shallow seas on both sides of the North Atlantic. There are other species of smaller size and there is a second group of species known as snailfishes or sea-snails. These have flabby or jelly-like bodies covered with small spines instead of tubercles. One of them, the common sea-snail, is also found on both sides of the North Atlantic.

Clinging like a leech
Lumpsuckers spend much of their lives clinging to rocks or, in the smaller species, to other less solid supports, such as seaweeds. The description of the strength of the sea-hen's sucker given by Thomas Pennant in his *British Zoology*, written in the 18th century, cannot be bettered and is usually quoted. 'By means of this part it adheres with vast force to anything it pleases. As a proof of its tenacity, we have known that on flinging a fish of this species just caught into a pail of water, it fixed itself so firmly to the bottom that on taking the fish by the tail the whole pail was by that means lifted, though it held some gallons, and that without removing the fish from its hold.'

Eight months' fasting
The feeding habits of the lumpsucker have not been fully studied but apparently it feeds mainly on crustaceans. During the breeding season and even beyond it takes no food, so there is a period of fasting from April to November, during which time the stomach is distended with water. Dr J Travis Jenkins, in *The Fishes of the British Isles*, tells us that when the stomach is perforated the water spurts out violently and the stomach walls collapse.

Male nursemaids
The female lays up to 136 000 pink eggs in April, on the shore between mid-tide and low-water marks. So at every tide they are uncovered for a period of time. The eggs are not in a solid mass but spread over a rock surface, and are guarded by the male. While they are covered with water he fans them with his pectoral fins to ensure that eggs in the centre of a clump will be fully aerated. He probably eats or otherwise removes any infertile or diseased eggs. In due course, the time being as yet uncertain, the eggs hatch and the tadpole-like larvae, as active as the parents are sluggish, swim around. They rest at intervals holding on with their sucker and wrapping the tail round their large head so they look like anything but a fish.

Come hell or high water

So far the story of the lumpsucker seems to be one of large numbers of eggs and larvae guarded securely by a male parent with an unusual sense of responsibility. In fact, the reverse is true. When the tide is out the eggs are eaten by gulls, crows, rooks, starlings and rats. When the tide is in they are eaten by a variety of fishes. Once the surviving eggs have hatched the larvae must face the same dangers. The male guarding the eggs may be attacked by crows and rooks or be torn from his perch by spring storms and battered on the rocks or be cast well up the beach, where he will die.

On one occasion watch was kept on a particular male lumpsucker for several weeks. Day after day, each time the tide went out, there was the lumpsucker at his post. The experiment was then tried of removing the lumpsucker and putting him a couple of yards from his eggs. He immediately wriggled back to take up position for guarding the eggs. When taken to a greater distance he still struggled back as soon as he could and fixed himself by his sucker in his former position with his snout almost touching the nearest eggs. On another occasion it was the eggs that were removed, by stormy waves that flung them well up the beach. When the storm subsided the father lumpsuckers were seen moving about over the shore, presumably searching for the lost eggs.

We always say the male lumpsucker is guarding the eggs. He is doing nothing of the kind. This sort of language is a relic of the times, two centuries or so ago, when naturalists first wrote about it. And writers since have slavishly copied them. A lumpsucker has no means of defending his eggs. He cannot even defend himself. What he does is to aerate the eggs. In the execution of this duty he has a built-in impulse to stand by the eggs no matter what happens. This much we can admire and marvel at the extraordinary instinct that pins him to his post even at the cost of his own life. We should stop saying he is guarding the eggs though unless we say he is guarding them against the danger of lack of oxygen. But this story of the lumpsucker is a first-class example of parental devotion.

class	**Osteichthyes**
order	**Scorpaeniformes**
family	**Cyclopteridae**
genus & species	***Cyclopterus lumpus*** *others*

△ *Part of the eggs of spawn laid by an Australian lungfish. Spawning is mainly in September and November. The development of the embryos is more similar to that of the frog tadpole than a fish.*

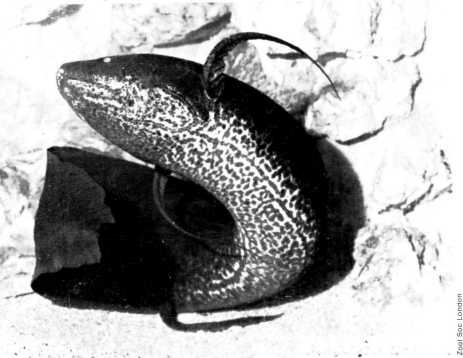

△ *The African lungfish has small embedded scales and very narrow pectoral and pelvic fins.*
▽ *The South American lungfish has an eel-like body, also with embedded scales, and slender fins.*

Lungfish

The earliest fossils of lungfishes go back over 350 million years. These and other fossils show that lungfishes have at some time or other lived all over the world. Today only 6 species survive: one in Australia, four in tropical Africa and one in South America. Having lungs for breathing air they can live in stagnant water. Some of them can also survive the drying out of rivers. The lungs are essentially pouched branches from the gut which in most fishes have modified into flotation organs or swimbladders (see diagrams on p. 591). Modifications and improvements in their efficiency during the course of evolution have led to the true lungs of active land animals.

The Australian lungfish Neoceratodus is the most primitive of the six. Originally it was found only in the Burnett and Mary Rivers in Queensland but has since been introduced to lakes and reservoirs in that state. Its alternative name, Burnett salmon, shows that it is a full-bodied fish and it may be as much as 6 ft long and 100 lb weight, although usually only half that length. The body is covered with large scales and the paired fins are flipper-like. The largest African lungfish Protopterus measures 7 ft but is usually 2—3 ft. Like the South American species Lepidosiren, the African lungfishes have more eel-like bodies with small scales embedded in the skin. The paired fins of Protopterus are long, slender and flexible, those of Lepidosiren are short and slender. The four African species range over a wide area of tropical Africa, the South American lungfish is widely distributed over the Amazon basin.

Buried in mud

The African and South American species have a pair of lungs and they must gulp air to live no matter how good the water they are living in. The South American lungfish tunnels into the mud as the stream dries out in summer and two of the African species burrow into the mud and give out quantities of slime which hardens to form a cocoon with a hole in the upper end. This resting state in hot weather, the reverse of hibernation, is called aestivation. During aestivation the fish continues to breathe at a reduced rate. The cocoon of the African lungfish, embedded in mud, has an opening to the surface and the fish lies doubled up with its head and tail at the lower end of this 'breathing tube'. While aestivating the lungfish absorbs its own muscles for food, and one examined before and after 6 months resting had dropped from $13\frac{1}{5}$ to $10\frac{1}{5}$ oz and its length had decreased from 16 to $14\frac{3}{8}$ in. Once out of aestivation it had more than made good these losses in 2 months.

Another problem for the lungfish is the disposal of body waste. Its kidneys separate water from urea—the poisonous end product of food breakdown—the water goes back into circulation and the urea is stored.

△ *The Australian lungfish, unlike the other two types, has a flatter and broader body covered with very large overlapping scales. The paired fins are broad and powerful and capable of supporting the fish by resting them on the bottom of a stream or pool.*

In most vertebrates 10 parts per million of urea in the system would be fatal. A lungfish can survive 20 000 parts per million. As soon as aestivation is over the urea is discharged and the kidneys cleared of it in a few hours.

The fish comes out of its cocoon when the rains return and the streams fill up once more. Usually the aestivation lasts only a few months, but African lungfishes dug out still in their cocoons embedded in a block of dried mud have been kept for over 4 years before being immersed once again in water. Although emaciated they soon recovered and began to feed.

The Australian lungfish has only one lung and lives in water with plenty of oxygen so does not need to come to the surface to gulp air. Moreover, it cannot survive drought and dies if kept out of water for any length of time.

A taste for snails

The Australian lungfish eats both animal and plant food, the others are carnivorous and the plant food they take is swallowed by accident as they grub for crustaceans and molluscs. A detailed study has been made of the food of one species of African lungfish by Philip S Corbet. This shows that the bulk of its food when fully grown is freshwater snails. It also takes a fair proportion of insect larvae and a small number of cichlid fishes. Moreover, the diet alters with size. Up to a foot long the lungfish eats insect larvae only, from then until it is 2 ft long its food is a mixture of insect larvae, snails and the occasional cichlid, but beyond 2 ft, it eats only snails.

Tadpole-like babies

The primitive state of the Australian lungfish is also seen in its breeding. The female lays her eggs at random among water plants and neither parent pays any further attention to them. Both African and South American species dig a cavity in the mud in which the female lays some 5 000 eggs. The male tends these, wriggling his body to drive over currents of water to aerate them. He also chases away anything coming near the nest. The larvae hatching from the eggs climb up the sides of the nest cavity and hang vertically with the head upwards for

1–2 months. The larvae have four pairs of external gills which they gradually lose. The first pair is lost at the end of the first month, the rest being lost during the next month in the South American lungfish while the African species take several months to lose theirs. The larva of the Australian lungfish does not have external gills. The other species grow their permanent gills as their larval gills are being absorbed. In one African species vestiges of external gills persist through life. The South American species has 6 gill arches and 5 gill clefts. The African species have 5 arches and 4 clefts.

The pelvic fins of the male of the South American lungfish grow filaments during the breeding season. These contain many small blood vessels. Opinion is divided on whether these give out oxygen to help the developing eggs or whether they act as extra gills, helping him to stay with the eggs rather than rise for air so often.

Snacks for the crocodiles

One of the main advantages for a fish to be able to live in stagnant waters is that there will be few enemies to contend with. That the present day lungfishes have persisted more or less unchanged for millions of years suggests that they have not had great pressure from predators. The main losses are among the young, and some of these may be from adult lungfishes themselves, especially in the African species which are apt to be pugnacious even to fishes their own size, judging from their behaviour in aquaria and the way they attack other fishes when netted. The adults are eaten by crocodiles as well as by fish eagles (p. 917) who take them as they come to the surface to gulp air.

Blocked nostrils

Land-living vertebrates breathe by lungs and take in air through the nostrils. The nose acts, therefore, as an organ of smell and supplies a passage for air used in breathing. Fishes have nostrils and a sense of smell. Most of them have no lungs, so the nostrils lead into blind cavities containing the olfactory (smell) membranes. Water is drawn in and driven out, merely to bathe the olfactory membrane. It had long been assumed that lungfishes, which have nostrils and lungs, breathed through their noses. Less than 20 years ago JW Atz showed that they did not. Among other things, when a lungfish breathes air it swims strongly to the surface, pushes its snout well out, opens its mouth wide and movements of the mouth and throat show it is swallowing air.

class	**Osteichthyes**
order	**Ceratodontiformes**
family	**Ceratodontidae**
genus & species	*Neoceratodus forsteri*
family	**Protopteridae**
genus & species	*Protopterus aethiopicus others*
family	**Lepidosirenidae**
genus & species	*Lepidosiren paradoxa*

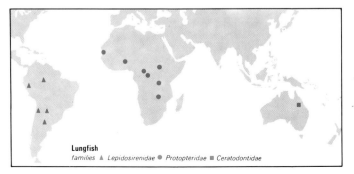

Lungfish
families ▲ *Lepidosirenidae* ● *Protopteridae* ■ *Ceratodontidae*

The six species of lungfish were once more widely spread but are now confined to three countries. One in Australia, one in South America and four in Africa very similar in form to the American species suggesting there was once a land link between continents.

◁ *Long-tailed salamander: has a tail nearly twice as long as its body. It spends most of the day hidden under logs and stones.*

Lungless salamander

The name 'lungless salamander' covers 150 species of salamanders living in Tropical and North America that have neither lungs nor gills but breathe through their skin and the lining of the mouth. A further peculiarity is that some of them cannot open their lower jaw to the normal gape. There is only one species outside America, represented by three subspecies in France, Italy and Sardinia.

Lungless salamanders range in size from $1\frac{1}{2}$ to $8\frac{1}{2}$ in. A few live permanently in water but most of them spend their lives on land. They are mainly sombrely coloured—black, grey or brown—but some have patches of red and the redbacked salamander occurs in 2 colour phases: red and grey with the belly of each spotted black and white. Varying proportions of red and grey individuals are found in any batch of larvae. Most lungless salamanders have the usual salamander shape, a long rounded body, tail about the same length and short legs, the front legs with 4 toes, the back legs with 5. The four-toed lungless salamander has 4 toes on each foot. The longtailed salamander is so called because its 7in. tail dwarfs a 4in. body. The California slender salamander is snakelike, with vestigial legs, and lies under fallen logs, coiled up tightly like a watch-spring.

Some species are widespread. The dusky salamander ranges over the eastern United States from New Brunswick southwards to Georgia and Alabama and westwards to Oklahoma and Texas. Other species are very localised. The Ocoee salamander lives in damp crevices in rocks or on the water-fall-splashed faces of rocks in Ocoee Gorge, southeast Tennessee. One of the European subspecies lives in southeast France and north Italy, the second lives in Tuscany, the third in Sardinia.

From deep wells to tall trees

Lungless salamanders mostly live in damp places, under stones or logs, among moss, under leaf litter, near streams or seepages or even in surface burrows in damp soil. The shovel-nosed salamander lives in mountain streams all its life, hiding under stones by day. Others live on land but go into water to escape enemies. The pygmy salamander, 2 in. long, living in the mountains of Virginia and North Carolina, can climb the rough bark of trees to a height of several feet. The arboreal salamander does even better, climbing trees to a height of 60 ft, sometimes making its home in old birds' nests. The Californian flatheaded salamander uses webbed feet to walk over slippery rocks and swings its tail from side to side as it walks, to help itself up a slope. On descent its curled tail acts as a brake.

Several species live in caves or artesian and natural wells as much as 200 ft deep. All are blind, one retains its larval gills throughout life and one cave species spends its larval life in mountain streams but migrates to underground waters before metamorphosis. It then loses its sight.

Creeping, crawling food

All lungless salamanders eat small invertebrates. Those living in water feed mainly on aquatic insect larvae. Those on land hunt slugs, worms, woodlice and insect larvae. One group of lungless salamanders *Plethodon* are known as woodland salamanders. They live in rocky crevices or in holes underground and eat worms, beetles and ants. The slimy salamander also eats worms, hard-shelled beetles, ants and centipedes as well as shieldbugs, despite their obnoxious odour and unpalatable flavour. The European species catches food with a sticky tongue which it can push out 1 inch.

Kissing salamanders

There is as much diversity in their breeding as in the way they live. Some lay their eggs in water and the larvae are fully aquatic;

others lay them on land, and among this second group are species in which the females curl themselves round their batches of 2–3 dozen eggs as if incubating. In a few species the female stays near her eggs until they hatch, but without incubating them or giving them any special care. The woodland salamanders lay their eggs in patches of moss or under logs and the larvae metamorphose before leaving the eggs. A typical species is the dusky salamander. The male deposits his sperm in a capsule or spermatophore. He then rubs noses with the female. A gland on his chin gives out a scent that stimulates the female to pick up the spermatophore with her cloaca. Her eggs are laid in clusters of two dozen in spring or early summer under logs or stones. Each egg is $\frac{3}{16}$ in. diameter and the larvae on hatching are $\frac{5}{8}$ in. long. It has external gills and goes into water, where it lives until the following spring, when it metamorphoses. The adults, $5\frac{1}{4}$ in. long, are dark brown or grey. When it first metamorphoses

the young salamander is brick-red and light cream in patches. Later it takes on the colours of the fully grown adult but has a light band down the back and a light line from the eye to the angle of the jaw.

Not so defenceless

Lungless salamanders, like other salamanders and newts, seldom have defensive weapons, a possible exception being the arboreal salamander with its fang-like teeth in the lower jaw. It is known to bite a finger when handled. The slimy salamander gives out a very sticky, glutinous secretion from its skin when handled and this possibly deters predators. The enemies are small snakes and frogs, which take their toll of the larvae and the young salamanders. It may be in an attempt to evade such enemies that the dusky salamander sometimes leaps about, several inches at a jump. The yellow blotched salamander, of California, has a curious behaviour that may be defensive. It raises itself on the tips of its toes, rocks its

body backwards and forwards, arches its tail and swings it from side to side. It also gives out a milky astringent fluid from the tail. And it squeaks like a mouse.

A special squeak

Peculiar features of these salamanders are that they lose their larval gills as they grow and they do not grow lungs. Instead, their skin has become the breathing organ with the skin lining the mouth acting the part of a lung by having a network of fine blood vessels in it, like the lining of a lung. The arboreal salamander has a similar network of fine blood vessels in the skin of its toes, which may play the part of lungs (or should they be called terrestrial gills?). Another extraordinary feature is that others, like the yellow-blotched salamander, squeak, although they have neither lungs nor voice box. They do this by contracting the throat to force air through the lips or nose.

class	**Amphibia**
order	**Caudata**
family	**Plethodontidae**
genera & species	**Aneides lugubris** *arboreal salamander*
	Batrachoseps attenuatus *California slender salamander*
	Desmognathus fuscus *dusky salamander*
	D. ocoee *Ocoee salamander*
	D. wrighti *pygmy salamander*
	Ensatina croceator *yellow-blotched salamander*
	Eurycea longicauda *long-tailed salamander*
	Hemidactylium scutatum *four-toed salamander*
	Leurognathus marmoratus *shovel-nosed salamander*
	Plethodon cinereus *red-backed salamander*
	P. glutinosus *slimy salamander*

Constance P Warner

△ Mountain salamander, **Desmognathus ochrophaeus** *lives near springs and streams where the ground is saturated.*

▷ *Red-backed salamander, occupant of old garden plots where there are tree stumps, rotting logs and moisture-conserving debris.*

AB Klots

Lynx

Lynxes are bobtailed members of the cat family and one, the bobcat, which stands somewhat apart from the others, has been separately dealt with (p. 389), as has the caracal or desert lynx (p. 506).

The original animal to be given this name, now distinguished as the European lynx, is up to $3\frac{1}{2}$ ft long in the head and body with an 8in. tail, weighing up to 40 lb. It has a relatively short body, tufted ears and cheek ruffs, powerful limbs and very broad feet. Its fur varies from a pale sandy-grey to rusty red and white on the underparts. Its summer coat is thin and poor, with black spots, its winter coat being dense and soft and usually lacking the spots. It ranges through the wooded parts of Europe, except south of a line from the Pyrenees and Alps. In Asia it extends eastwards to the Pacific coast of Siberia and southwards to the Himalayas.

Closely related to it is the Spanish lynx, which is smaller, with shorter and more heavily spotted fur. The Canada lynx is larger, has longer hair and is often without spots.

*The latest view of many leading zoologists is that lynx types all constitute one species **Lynx lynx,** but for the moment we are following the accepted pattern.*

Champion walkers

Lynxes live in forests, especially of pine, which they seldom leave. They are solitary beasts, hunting by night, using sight and smell. Their keen sight is proverbial and is summed up in the way we describe anyone with keen eyes or keen powers of observation as lynx-eyed. Ancient writers credited the lynx with being able to see through a stone wall. Lynxes run very little but are tireless walkers, following scent trails relentlessly for miles to pursue their prey. Alternatively, as they climb trees well, lynxes will lie out on branches to drop on to passing prey, or will lie in ambush. They swim well, and their broad feet carry them over soft ground or over snow. The voice is a caterwauling similar to that of a domestic tomcat but louder, and like a cat a lynx uses claws and teeth in a fight. Within its home range a lynx buries its urine and faeces but near the boundary of this range both are deposited on prominent places, such as hillocks. These serve as boundary marks to be recognized by the occupant and by neighbours.

Instant death

Lynxes used to be numerous in Europe where today, in most parts, they are scarce, having been wiped out because of their alleged raids on sheep, goats and other livestock. Some zoologists claim that lynxes are less interested in farmstock than in wild game. The natural food of the European

Feline ferocity: the Canadian lynx hunts at night in pine forests, using sight and smell to track down prey such as the snowshoe rabbit.

roebild

Lagomorph meal: death is quick as the lynx bites into the shoulders and then the nape.

Mating takes place in March, the young being born after a gestation of 63 days in the European lynx and after 60 in the Canada lynx. The litter is usually 2–4 kittens born well furred but blind. The eyes open at 10 days and the kittens are weaned at 2 months but remain with the mother for another 7 months. Although the kittens are somewhat advanced at birth they are slow in developing. Even at 8 months or more they still have milk teeth and their claws are still feeble. The young lynx must therefore feed on small rodents or on food killed by the mother. Should it become separated from its mother when the first winter snows fall its chances of survival are slim, with the small rodents living under 2 ft or more of snow. The females mature at a year old and the recorded life span is up to 20 years.

Driven out of house and home

Man is the only enemy of the lynx but his hand has been heavy. Lynx fur has long been valued for garments and trimmings. A gown of crimson damask furred with lynx is listed in an inventory of the belongings of the Duke of Richmond, taken in 1527. In Canada, lynx fur was prominent in the transactions of the Hudson Bay Company. More than hunting, the destruction of forests in Europe and in Canada, or, as in Europe, the husbanding of forests, has deprived the lynx of its best and most natural habitat. In Sweden, for example, hunting and changes in the forest drove the lynx northwards during the 19th century until what had been the northern limit of its range became the southern limit. This meant less food and, more important, less chance of survival for the kittens with the longer and more rigorous winters in the higher latitudes. Finally, in 1928, the Swedish lynx was given legal protection. Its numbers have since begun to rise and the lynxes have moved farther south.

class	**Mammalia**
order	**Carnivora**
family	**Felidae**
genus & species	***Lynx canadensis*** *Canada lynx* ***L. lynx*** *European lynx* ***L. pardellus*** *Spanish lynx*

lynx includes hares, rabbits, ground birds and small deer. The latter are killed by a bite at the nape of the neck which severs the spinal cord, or the lynx may use a two-way bite, into the shoulders and then into the nape. Death is instantaneous with both methods. Lynxes also kill squirrels, foxes, badgers, fish, beetles, especially the wood-boring species, and many small rodents. They tend to kill small game such as rodents in summer, turning to larger game such as deer in winter. The prey of the Canada lynx is similar. The snowshoe rabbit, one of the North American hares, is its main prey (see p. 1153).

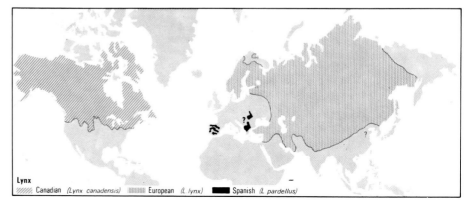

Lynx
//// Canadian *(Lynx canadensis)* ‖‖‖‖ European *(L. lynx)* ■ Spanish *(L. pardellus)*

Lyrebird

In 1798 the early explorers of the mountain forests of eastern Australia found what they called a mountain pheasant. It was also called Native Pheasant and New South Wales bird-of-paradise. It was not until the 1820's that the name lyrebird came into use.

The male lyrebird has a body the size of a bantam cockerel, with strong legs and feet. His plumage is ash-brown tinged with red on the wings. His 2ft tail is made up of 16 feathers. The two outer feathers are broad and shaped like the frame of a lyre. The remaining feathers lying between them are delicate lacelike plumes. The female has a similar plumage but with an ordinary tail. Males do not grow the distinctive tail until they are 3 years old.

Stage-struck

In mountain forests where the rocky slopes, running down to fast flowing streams, are covered with large tree ferns, the almost legendary lyrebirds act out their unique and inspiring display. In the autumn each male lays claim to a territory of 3–6 acres. With his strong legs and feet he scrapes together large mounds of earth and leaves on which to display. He may make a dozen of these in his territory. Having sung from the top of a log or from a low branch of a tree as a preliminary he flies to the top of one of the mounds and begins to sing in a loud penetrating voice. After a few minutes he unfolds his tail feathers which he has so far carried like a peacock's train. He raises these and swings them forward over his back, like a canopy, the two outer broad feathers that form the frame being swung out until they are at right angles to the body. Half-hidden under this shimmering canopy he begins to dance, pouring out a torrent of bubbling notes. The song rises higher and higher then suddenly stops. The tail is swung back into the normal position and the male lyrebird walks away, his display finished. Sometimes he will shake his tail feathers violently while they are spread over his back, making clicks and drumming noises at the same time.

People have written about this display being performed for the benefit of the hen, but there is little to suggest that it is more than a matter of advertising his possession of a territory.

One-chick family

Mating is during May to July, when the hen alone takes 3–4 weeks to build a large nest of sticks, lining it with moss. The male is polygamous and gives no help. The nest is roofed and may be built on the ground, on a rocky ledge, an old tree stump or in a high tree fork. In this she lays one greyish-purple egg about the size of a domestic hen's egg, having deserted the nest for several days. She deserts the egg for several days also, but when she begins to incubate it she does so for 6 weeks. The downy chick hatching from it loses its down in 10 days and begins to grow feathers but does not leave the nest for 6 weeks from hatching.

Graham Pizzey

Superb lyrebird sings in Sherbrooke forest, 26 miles from Melbourne, Victoria.

During that time the hen brings insects and snails to feed it. Adult lyrebirds feed by scratching the ground with their strong toes and claws, like domestic chickens, for seeds, insects and other small invertebrates.

Traffic in tails

The adult lyrebird has no large natural enemies although it is likely the thylacine or Tasmanian wolf may have preyed on it before being exterminated. One enemy is the introduced red fox. The chief danger is from snakes, large lizards, and birds like the kookaburra raiding the nest. The only other enemy is man, whose raids are now curbed as the bird is protected by law. As soon as the lyrebird had been discovered a demand arose for its beautiful tail-feathers, and even in the early years of this century the tails were still being hawked around the streets of Sydney by the basketful. AH Chisholm, the Australian ornithologist, tells us that one Sydney dealer sold 498 tails in 1911 and another had exported 800 in the same year. Another ornithologist declared that 2 000 tails had been exported in 3 years at about the same time, although their export was prohibited. Fortunately the bird has long been protected by law so its future is ensured.

Unnatural position of feathers appears on stamp.

An artist's error

The lyrebird figures on Australian seals and stamps with its lyre-shaped tail held upright. This it never does except for a brief moment when swinging the tail from the train position to the canopy position over its back. Whether the person who designed the stamp had only the tail of the bird, which he stood against the wall of his studio to draw, or whether this was the only way to get the whole bird on to a vertical stamp, is unknown. Tradition dies hard, however, and even now artists are still drawing the lyrebird with his tail held in this unnatural position.

Alarm-raising mimic

The fame of the lyrebird rests not only on its remarkable tail but also on its voice. Its natural song is one of beauty and power and those who have heard it in the fern-covered glades of eastern Australia are loud in its praise. The bird is also an accomplished mimic. It has even been called Australia's mockingbird and at least one Australian zoologist was prepared to argue that nowhere in the world is there a bird mimic to touch it. Lyrebirds have been heard to imitate the crack of the whipbird, the chant of the pilotbird, the melody of the grey thrush and the screams of cockatoos. They will mimic a chorus of cockatoos, even to the whirring of their wings, or the solitary voice of a tiny sparrow. There seems the possibility that these mimickings are learned by young lyrebirds from their parents, and the suggestion has been made that some of the lyrebirds' notes are songs of extinct birds passed on from generation to generation. Certainly lyrebirds are unusual in using mimicked songs to answer each other.

Lyrebirds also mimic mechanical sounds, such as the rattling of chains and the sounds of a saw, as well as human speech. Chisholm tells of a timber mill in Victoria where three blasts of a whistle were used to signal an accident and six blasts meant a fatality. One day six blasts were heard and men came running from all directions. It was a lyrebird that had heard the three blasts, which were not infrequent, had copied them, and one day repeated them in succession.

△ *Threat display by female at intruder.*

▽ *Shimmering feather canopy as a male displays.*

class	**Aves**
order	**Passeriformes**
family	**Menuridae**
genus & species	*Menura novaehollandiae*

Macaque

The macaques are the most numerous and widespread of the Old World monkeys. They are found in the tropical forests of Southeast Asia, the scrublands of India, the snowy mountains of Tibet, the temperate forests of Japan, and the Atlas mountains of North Africa. They include forms with long tails, short tails and no tail at all. Most are brown, but some are black. They are larger and longer-faced than guenons, but smaller and shorter-faced than baboons. They are, in fact, hard to define. Two species, the Barbary 'ape' and the pigtailed monkey, are dealt with in separate entries.

Of the remainder, the best known is the rhesus monkey, $1\frac{1}{2}$–2 ft long with a tail less than a foot long, brown with much brighter, more reddish hindparts as if wearing orange-coloured trousers. Its face is pink. Rhesus monkeys are found in northern India west to Afghanistan, east to North Vietnam, south to central Burma and Thailand, north to the Yangtze River and Lake Kukunor, with some around Pekin. South of the Godavari River, India, the bonnet macaque replaces the rhesus, and in Sri Lanka the toque monkey. These two are smaller, under 20 in. long, with tails nearly 2 ft long. They are entirely brown, with pink faces and with a 'cap' of radiating hairs on the head, which in the bonnet monkey is short, leaving the forehead bare. To the east, the rhesus monkey is replaced by the crab-eating monkey, in southern Burma and Thailand, Malaya, Indonesia and the Philippines; this too is small and long-tailed, but has no cap on the crown. An allied species lives in Taiwan. In the Himalayas, and more or less wherever the rhesus is found, but higher up the mountains, is the large, pale, fawn Assam macaque.

Another group of macaques have very short tails, or none at all. The stump tail is a grotesque-looking monkey with short, stout limbs and a bright red face which turns blotchy brown in the sunlight. Old ones go bald, beginning at the forehead. The Tibetan macaque is larger, shaggy and bearded, with a brown face. The Japanese macaque is almost as big, also shaggy, but with a long, mournful pink face. The Celebes macaques are a world of diversity all by themselves, ranging from the jet-black, long-faced 'black ape' of the northern peninsula of Celebes, with a backward-drooping crest of hair on its crown and pink, kidney-shaped ischial callosities – the patches of hard skin on the rump – to the brown, short-faced, restless Moor macaque of the south of Celebes. And there is a chain of intermediate forms between these two closely related species of macaque found in the Celebes islands.

Okapia

With a topknot looking like a poor man's wig a toque macaque looks around its leafy home.

Counting heads

When two macaque troops meet, there is always some kind of conflict. Normally, if two troops' home ranges overlap, the timetables of daily movement are geared so they do not meet, but if the smaller troop is unwary and fails to see the bigger troop coming, they will probably be attacked. Subordinate males generally begin the fight, which can last up to twenty minutes and result in scratches and bruises, rarely anything more serious.

All macaques live in large social groups, made up of all ages and both sexes. The exact size and composition of the group varies from place to place and from species to species. In sparse parts of forest and scrubland, even in towns and by railways or roadsides in India rhesus monkey troops number 10–25. In more fertile country, as in the eastern Sunderbans, the Corbett National Park and around temples – where they are protected and even fed – troops of 30–60 are common. Bonnet monkeys live in rather larger troops, 25–30 in poor wild environments and 50–60 in rich cultivated areas. Crab-eaters live in troops of approximately the same size or slightly larger – one of 73 was counted in the Singapore Botanic Garden. The largest troops of all are found among Japanese macaques, whose average troop size is 194 – anything up to 570 in a single troop is known. Japanese scientists began to feed troops of Japanese macaques in 1952 in order to be able to study them. Since then troop size has increased.

Macaques — monkeys with caps, bonnets and manes

◁ *Delightful scene of a young Japanese macaque suckling. Their bond may last for life. Note the infant's fur is much darker than the mother's.*

▽◁ *Bonnet monkeys of southern India get their names from the quaint cap of radiating hair on the crown of the head.*

▽ *The lion-tailed macaque is the least typical of macaques and perhaps the least well known of the group. It lives in dense forest regions of the mountains near the west coast of southern India and is said to be shy and retiring, unlike many macaques. It is identified by the lion-like tail tuft and the pale face ruff which is more exaggerated in the male (illustrated).*

Kojo Tanaka

Popperfoto

Okapia

△ *Black 'ape' playmates. This monkey has a tail so considerably reduced that it does not show outside its body. This accounts for its name as no true ape has a tail. In the northern part of its native island—the Celebes—it is regarded by the local inhabitants as sacred ancestors of their own tribe. The black macaque is distinguished from the similar moor macaque of the south of Celebes, by the head crest and by the ridges on the upper sides of the muzzle, which leads it to be mistaken for a baboon.*

△▷ *Space monkeys: a rhesus monkey was the first primate to be shot into the stratosphere in a rocket. It is the best known of this group as it is extensively used in biological laboratories for experimental purposes. The Rh blood factor was first demonstrated in rhesus monkeys.*

▷ *Young Japanese wrestlers: Japanese macaques are born between April and September, the peak being in June and July. In the macaque species breeding is seasonal in areas where there is marked variation in food supply, and year round where there is not.*

In rhesus, crab-eater and Assam macaque troops there are 2 or 3 females to every male. In bonnet troops the numbers are about equal. At the troop centre is either a single dominant male or a coalition of two or more. Other males are ranked below the dominant ones. In one troop studied by Southwick, Beg and Siddiqi there was a central coalition of two males, and an external high-ranking male who was dominant over either of them separately, but subordinate when the two of them acted in concert. The 'coalition' custom is found in bonnets, too, but here the society is a little more relaxed, and a subordinate male is allowed to sit in the centre of the troop provided he makes the necessary lip-smacking gestures and 'presents' his hindquarters to the dominant males, as a sign of his submission. As far as is known, crab-eaters have an even rank-order with no coalition. In Japanese macaques subordinate males are pushed right out to the periphery, and may even live isolated, solitary lives.

Peaceful co-existence
Macaques share most of their range with langurs. There is no competition for food, the macaques being omnivorous and the langurs leaf-eaters. The two types of monkey co-exist peacefully, but the macaques are always dominant to the langurs.

High-born monkeys
Breeding is seasonal in areas where there is marked variation in food supply, year-round where there is not. In Jaipur there are two birth seasons, March–May and September–October for rhesus monkeys, while bonnets show a birth peak in February and March. In Japanese macaques there is a peak in June and July, and no births at all outside April–September. Sexual behaviour varies; in rhesus monkeys a female in season forms a 'consort pair' with a male, usually beginning with a dominant one. The pair move around and forage together and groom each other. The association lasts from a few hours to a few days.

Gestation is about six months, the young being born with eyes closed but opening within two hours. Hair in the newborn is mainly confined to the head and back. The infant fur is usually darker than the adult's, so he is noticeable at a distance. Male macaques take quite an interest in the infants, and tolerate their play. This fatherly attitude is especially marked among Japanese macaques. The mother to offspring bond seems to continue throughout life and the offspring of a mother who is of high dominance rank tend to inherit high rank within the group.

Food for many predators
Macaques are preyed upon by leopards, smaller cats, wild dogs, eagles, pythons, crocodiles and even by monitor lizards. Human interference varies from place to place. In India, though not held sacred like langurs, macaques bask in a kind of reflected glory and are usually not molested. In temples, people often feed them. Everywhere, however, thousands, mainly youngsters, are exported to medical laboratories in Europe and the United States.

Sitting comfortably — a long tailed macaque.

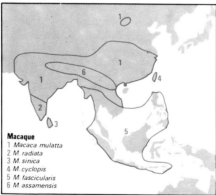

Macaque
1 *Macaca mulatta*
2 *M. radiata*
3 *M. sinica*
4 *M. cyclopis*
5 *M. fascicularis*
6 *M. assamensis*

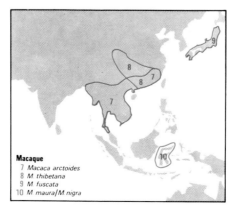

Macaque
7 *Macaca arctoides*
8 *M. thibetana*
9 *M. fuscata*
10 *M. maura/M. nigra*

Blueprints for man

Macaques do well in captivity and individuals of several species have survived more than 20 years in zoos. They are easily fed, do not mope and take a lively interest in all that goes on around them. This is not such an asset as it appears and it may well lead to their extermination in the wild. Medical research depends to an unhappily great extent on experiments with live animals and primates are the most valuable of all animals for this because they are so closely related to man. Experiments performed on rats or dogs are much less likely to be applicable to man than experiments on monkeys. A most notable vindication of research on primates was the development of the Salk vaccine, against polio.

Ideally, the great apes would be the 'blueprints for man'. Results of any experiments on them would almost certainly be the same as for man, but gorillas, chimpanzees and orang-utans are rare and difficult to obtain. The Old World monkeys are the next closest to man, and among these the macaques are the most suitable. They are, therefore, imported by the thousand every year. Dr Cliff Jolly has revealed a shocking story of exploitation. The numbers of macaques imported into Europe and the United States for use in laboratories has risen yearly. By 1965 the annual 'consumption' of primates was put at a quarter of a million. Many wild populations are already showing signs of drastic reduction as a result. The young are easiest to catch, and live longest in the laboratory. One result is that troops of rhesus macaques living near human habitation consist of only 6–10% of juveniles, instead of the normal 25% necessary for maintaining the population.

Another scandalous situation is the lack of breeding programmes. If an adequate number of monkeys are born in captivity then—given an economical use of experimental animals—there need be no trapping in the wild and no drain on wild populations. But such is not the case. In 1966 more than 60 000 monkeys were used in experiments in the United States alone. Of these only 4 070 were bred by the institutions concerned—all the rest were imported, mainly rhesus and crab-eaters. It is to be hoped that in an age increasingly concerned with conservation the primate resources will also receive their fair share of attention.

class	**Mammalia**
order	**Primates**
family	**Cercopithecidae**
genus & species	***Macaca sinica*** toque monkey
	M. assamensis Assamese macaque
	M. cyclopis Formosan macaque
	M. fascicularis crab-eating monkey
	M. fuscata Japanese macaque
	M. maura Moor macaque
	M. mulatta rhesus monkey
	M. nigra Celebes black ape
	M. radiata bonnet monkey
	M. arctoides stumptail monkey
	M. thibetana Tibetan macaque

Macaw

The 18 species of macaw include the largest and most colourful members of the parrot family. They live in tropical America, from southern Mexico through Central America to Paraguay. They have large beaks, the upper mandible being long and strongly hooked. The skin on the cheeks and around the eyes is naked except for a scattering of very small feathers.

The largest is the scarlet or red and blue macaw, of Mexico to Bolivia, 3 ft long, of which 2 ft is tail. It is mainly scarlet except for the yellow wing coverts and the blue of the flight feathers, the lower back feathers and outer tail feathers. The blue and yellow macaw, ranging from Panama to Paraguay, is only slightly smaller. It is a rich blue on the crown, nape, back, wings and upperside of tail, golden yellow on the underside, including the underside of the tail. There is a large black patch on the throat, the bill is black and the white sides of the face are marked with black wavy lines. The military or great green macaw, 30 in. long and ranging from Mexico to Brazil, is green, shading to blue on flight feathers, rump and tail coverts, with a crimson band on the forehead and red on the upperside of the tail. Less gaudy but probably more beautiful, certainly more prized by fanciers, is the hyacinthine macaw, 34 in. long, a cobalt blue throughout its plumage. Its range is limited to the interior jungles of the Amazon basin. The smaller species are usually green.

Commuting parrots

Macaws move about in screeching flocks except when breeding. Their day starts with a screeching chorus as individual birds leave their roosts to gather in a tree. There they bask in the early morning sun before setting off to feed. As the midday heat builds up they seek the shade, but when the sun's rays begin to weaken they come out again to feed. At dusk they return to their assembly point, usually a bare tree, before dispersing to roost.

Steamhammer beaks

Most macaws feed on seeds, nuts and fruits, the larger of them cracking even hard-shelled nuts such as Brazil nuts with their beaks and extracting the kernels with the

▷ *Indignant blue and yellow macaw.*
▽ *Rendezvous at Felipe Benavides Fountain —
red and blue and blue and yellow macaws.*

beak helped by the fleshy tongue. Precise details of their feeding in the wild are hard to come by, but in captivity, although these form their basic foods, they seem to show a liking for such things as bread and butter and cake, and tame macaws have been known to take meat readily. It may be, therefore, that they take some insect food in the wild. This possibly explains, at least in part, their readiness to pull wooden structures to pieces, such as the edges of nesting boxes or woodwork frames in the aviary. In the wild the same activities would expose insect grubs.

Bashful male

Except for the hyacinthine macaw, which is said to nest in holes in earth banks, macaws nest in hollows in trees, sometimes high up from the ground. Once the eggs are laid macaws are aggressive towards anyone approaching their nest. Even tame macaws will defy their owners trying to see what is happening. A fairly clear account can, however, be given of the breeding behaviour of the blue and yellow macaw, based mainly on observations published by Mr Donald Risdon, in the *Avicultural Magazine* for 1965. He found little distinction between male and female except that the male blushes when excited, the bare skin of his face going a deep pink. The female seldom blushes and when she does the colour hardly shows. At the same time as he blushes the male nods his head up and down and contracts the pupils of his eyes. When Risdon's pair showed signs of breeding he gave them rotten wood, which they chewed up in typical macaw fashion. The eggs are slightly larger than pigeon's eggs. The nestling is still naked and blind at a week old. The wing quills begin to erupt at 4 weeks, the bill darkens and the eyes open. The back then begins to grow feathers followed by the tail and later the rest of the body and head, the young macaw becoming fully feathered by 10 weeks of age. It does not leave the nest for another 3 weeks, except to sit at the entrance. The parents feed it during this time by regurgitation. At 6 months the young macaw is as large as its parents and looks like them.

Extinct macaws

With so formidable a beak a macaw could be a match for most small predators. Its main enemy is the harpy eagle. Their habit of feeding in flocks combined with their garish colours have made macaws vulnerable to the South American Indians with their blowpipes and arrows. Even this persecution has probably left the birds' numbers unimpaired on the mainland but the red macaw of Jamaica has not been seen since 1765 and the green and yellow macaw of the same island became extinct in the early 19th century. The Guadeloupe red macaw became extinct a century before this and the Dominican green and yellow macaw in the late 18th century. The Martinique macaw has not been heard of since 1640 and then there was one which has been called the mysterious macaw. No specimen of this is known but a description of it was published in 1658 — and that is all we know of it except that it lived on 'one of the West Indian islands'.

Royal favourites

The elimination of so many species on West Indian islands suggests they were killed off by man, for food, possibly for their feathers, or for the young to be taken into captivity. There may have been other causes of which little is known. All we know for certain is that macaws were popular as pets—more truthfully, perhaps, they were 'status symbols'—in Europe from the 16th century.

class	**Aves**
order	**Psittaciformes**
family	**Psittacidae**
genera & species	***Anodorhynchus hyacinthinus*** *hyacinthine macaw* ***Ara ararauna*** *blue and yellow macaw* ***A. macao*** *scarlet macaw* ***A. militaris*** *military macaw, others*

◁ *Rhapsody in blue: hyacinthines preening.*
▽ *Red and blue macaw,* **Ara chloroptera.**

roebild

△ *Helped by their streamlined shape and powerful tail, shoals of mackerel move very fast as they scour the upper waters for food.*

DP Wilson

Mackerel

Diminutive relatives of the mighty tunas, mackerel share with them the streamlined shape, voracious feeding, and agile swimming which have made them favourites with anglers the world over.

The common European mackerel has a plump but streamlined body, blue green on the back, silvery below. The back is patterned with darker ripple marks, but two varieties are occasionally seen. In one, the dotted mackerel, the ripple marks are replaced by spots. In the other, the scribbled mackerel, the ripple marks are finer and look like marbling. There are two dorsal fins, the one in front being spiny, and the pelvic fins are well forward, almost level with the pectoral fins. A line of finlets runs from the second dorsal to the tail fin, with a similar row of finlets on the underside of the body.

The range of the common mackerel in the eastern Atlantic is from Norway to the Canaries. The same species occurs in the western Atlantic from Chesapeake Bay to the Gulf of Maine. The Spanish mackerel occurs in these same areas but does not extend so far north. The Pacific mackerel ranges from Alaska to the Gulf of California, and on the other side of the Pacific, with a similar distribution, is the Japanese mackerel.

*The pygmy mackerels live in the Indo-Australian region. These are similar fishes, more deep bodied and up to 15 in. long. **Rastrelliger kanagurta**, of the Indian Ocean, known as **kembong**, is fished in large numbers all the way round the coasts of the Indian Ocean from East Africa to the Malay Archipelago.*

The horse mackerel is not a mackerel but a member of the family Carangidae, although its habits are similar to those of true mackerel.

Marine merry-go-round

Mackerel live in shoals, but to a lesser extent than, for example, the herring. At the end of October they leave the surface waters, go to the bottom and lie densely packed in the troughs and trenches. Towards the end of December they spread outwards over the surrounding seabed. At the end of January they move up to the surface, coming together in shoals, and start moving towards the spawning grounds. One of the main spawning grounds is near the edge of the continental shelf, in a wide V to the south of Ireland. The period of spawning is from March to June, after which they move into inshore waters breaking up into small shoals, and they stay there until October, when they go down to the bottom again to repeat the cycle.

Seasonal change of diet

On the seabed, mackerel feed on shrimps and smaller crustaceans, marine bristle-worms and small fishes. When they return to the surface in January they change their diet, taking animal plankton, especially the copepod *Calanus*, selectively picking these from the water, snapping them up as a swallow snaps up flies. From June to October, while in inshore waters, the mackerel feed on small fishes, especially young herrings, sprats and sand eels. Mackerel hunt mainly by smell, as is shown by the Breton fishermen who lure them by pouring stale fish blood overboard and scooping up the mackerel attracted to it. They must use sight at close quarters, however. With their pelvic fins well forward they can turn in a tight circle to catch prey as fast as themselves but less manoeuvrable.

Sinking eggs

The female lays about half a million eggs, each $\frac{1}{20}$ in. diameter. Each egg has a small oil globule in it and floats at the surface for 2 days. Then it sinks slowly down to mid-water where it remains suspended for a short while. If the temperature is right, about 15°C/58°F, the egg hatches and a larval mackerel $\frac{1}{10}$ in. long, still bearing a yolk sac, is born. The yolk lasts for about

9 days, after which the young mackerel begins to hunt minute plankton. Mackerel take 2 years to mature, at about a foot long.

Important food fish

Mackerel are preyed upon by fast swimming predatory fishes, especially in the young stages, their first two years of life, about which little is known. They are caught in nets or on long lines, or by spinning. Mackerel are only second in importance to herring among pelagic fishes. They are caught in seine nets from March to June and by hook and line from July to October.

Diver's discovery

Dr J Travis Jenkins tells us that it is a belief among fishermen that the first mackerel of the season are blind, that they have a cloudy film of skin over the eyes, which disappears in summer. One reason for this belief is that mackerel will not take bait until the summer. It used to be thought by marine zoologists that mackerel strained plankton from the sea, as a whalebone whale does. This seemed reasonable because mackerel have slender gill-rakers beset with fine spines making an efficient filtering apparatus. Both these beliefs were corrected in 1921 when an officer of the Royal Navy was hanging below a ship in a diver's suit during salvage operations. In the shadow of the ship the plankton animals showed up in dark silhouette against the sunlit waters beyond. The mackerel appreciated this advantage and the diver was able to watch them distinctly snapping up individual copepods—at a time when they should have had a film over their eyes.

class	**Osteichthyes**
order	**Perciformes**
family	**Scombridae**
genus & species	***Scomber japonicus*** Spanish or chub ***S. scombrus*** common others

Madagascar

Madagascar

According to the classic definition of the world's regions of fauna, Madagascar is part of the Ethiopian region–which also includes Africa south of the Sahara–and there are too many biogeographical likenesses for this to be denied.

This said, Madagascar must nonetheless be seen as a very special sub-region. Isolated for millions of years it has preserved many archaic animals and also there are many groups absent that are widespread in distribution elsewhere. For instance, there are no true monkeys in Madagascar, but lemurs have developed supremely well. Apart from the fossa, there are no large carnivores and no ruminants, either. There are few freshwater species of fish. Moreover the island's reptiles are few in species and number, although chameleons are abundant.

A special climate

In many ways Madagascar forms a small, separate continent. Its natural framework provides it with all the variety of a great country–one that is dangerously threatened. As a result of man's intervention, flora and fauna are disappearing. Original forest has been alarmingly burnt out–and in some regions where it once existed there is now only savanna.

Madagascar is a massive island with inhospitable coasts (except for the north where there is a majestic bay). The bulk of its surface is taken up by a plateau 2600–4600 ft above sea level, which rises continuously towards the east and is dominated by extinct volcanoes. There are three main mountain ranges; in the north, the centre and the south. The northern range is more than 9200 ft high. The entire eastern mountainous border forms a front which receives the brunt of the wet easterly winds and juts out in plateaus over a straight coastal fringe of lagoons. All the lands to the west of the oceans have a strong trade wind climate. (This trade wind also blows on the eastern fronts of meridional and East Africa and a similar situation applies to the south-east coast of Brazil.)

A mountainous island like Madagascar, subject as it is to the trades, is wet on the sides of the mountains that face the wind, and dry on those sheltered from it. But the trade wind climate is extremely complex. The island alternately experiences the south-easterly trades in winter and the north-east monsoon in summer. Land and sea breezes also have a local influence on the release of rain. On the east coast a night-time wind off the land blows perpendicularly to the trades–and the meeting of these two winds results in rain at night.

All Madagascar's climate depends on the high pressure system of the Indian Ocean. The monsoon brings stormy winds, which are sometimes devastating. Cyclones often sweep the island. The south-west, however, sheltered from rain-carrying winds, experiences months of absolute dryness–and as a result is bush country. The north-east does not have trade winds but gets monsoon rains instead. This is savanna country. The Madagascan plateau itself only has rain in summer, but its lateritic soil provides a mediocre basis for life.

Animal populations

The highly specialized Madagascan fauna is poorly accounted for. It is generally believed that there was a process of filtration between the African mainland and the island. Certainly none of the larger mammals widely represented in Africa managed to cross. The initial populations consisted entirely of arboreal animals and small or medium-size ground-dwellers. It is thought that they came across on 'rafts', formed of bundles of trees uprooted by the action of great rivers; and, furthermore, that these animals came from one African basin alone–which explains the original peculiarity of the Madagascan fauna. Some of the lemurians later grew to considerable size and this is accounted for by the influence of isolation. The Madagascan bovids or wild cattle have certainly been imported. The wild pigs were also without doubt brought to the island by man.

Madagascar was probably linked to Africa until about the end of the Mezozoic era, since when it has remained isolated.

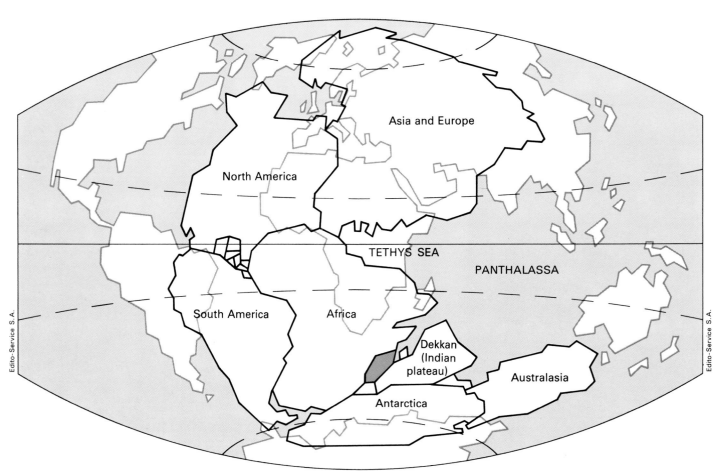

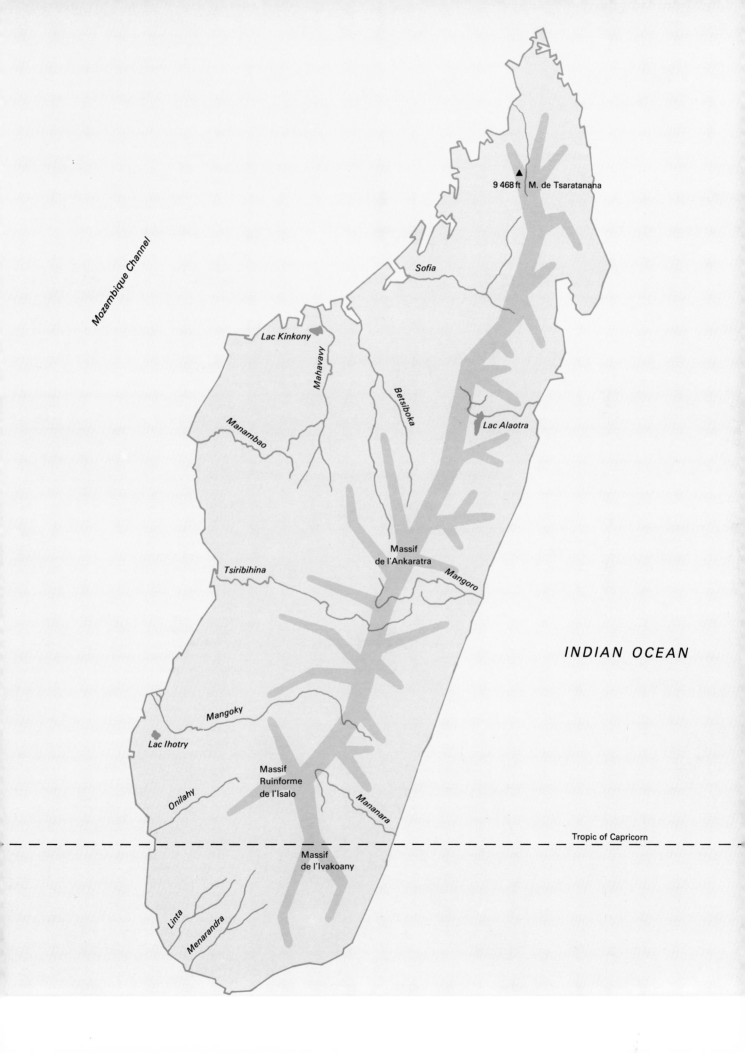

Mozambique Channel

9 468 ft ▲ M. de Tsaratanana

Sofia

Lac Kinkony

Mahavavy

Betsiboka

Lac Alaotra

Manambao

Massif
de l'Ankaratra

Mangoro

Tsiribihina

INDIAN OCEAN

Mangoky

Lac Ihotry

Massif
Ruinforme
de l'Isalo

Mananara

Onilahy

Tropic of Capricorn

Massif
de l'Ivakoany

Linta

Menarandra

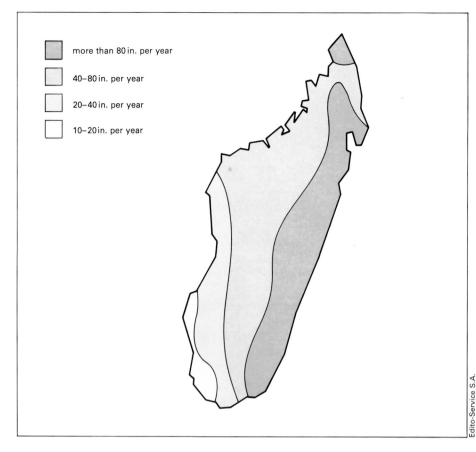

Madagascar is the fourth largest island in the world, and is in the equatorial and tropical zone. The rainfall becomes less abundant as it travels westward, the trade winds blowing from the east. Generally, there are two seasons, one dry (from May to October) and the other wet and hot. The driest regions are in the south and south-east, but the scrub and bush is completely different to that of Africa.

Legend (rainfall map):
- more than 80 in. per year
- 40–80 in. per year
- 20–40 in. per year
- 10–20 in. per year

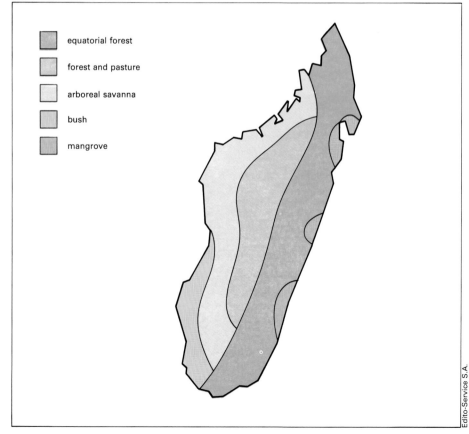

Legend (vegetation map):
- equatorial forest
- forest and pasture
- arboreal savanna
- bush
- mangrove

The lemuroids

The Madagascan prosimians (order Lemuroidea) are divided into three families–Lemuridae, Indridae and Daubentoniidae. Of these the Lemuridae, the lemur family, is by far the richest.

The Lemuridae are divided into two sub-families: Cheirogaleinae are very small lemurs which a lot of naturalists call mouse lemurs or dwarf lemurs; Lemurinae are large lemurs. All have evolved without having to compete with other higher primates which would probably force them from habitats. They have been able to adapt without being subjected to any great threats–and the result is a proliferation of forms.

The members of the sub-family Cheirogaleinae are only compared to mice on account of their size and not because they resemble them. They are more like monkeys–and even more like squirrels. There are three kinds of these little lemurs: the mouse lemurs (*Microcebus* spp), the dwarf lemurs (*Cheirogaleus* spp) and the fork-marked mouse lemur *Phaner furcifer*, which is the largest of the sub-family. There are also three genera of Lemurinae: gentle lemurs (*Hapalemur* spp), true lemurs (*Demur* spp) and sportive lemurs (*Lepilemur* spp). The family Lemuridae are unequally spread on the island, and sometimes form quite separate sub-species.

Mouse lemurs are essentially tree-dwellers and nocturnal. The sub-species of lesser mouse lemur *Microcebus murinus rufus*, lives in the rain forests of the east coast, while the other sub-species, *M. m. murinus*, lives in dry forests. Their body length is no more than 12 in. and their tail almost as long. They weigh around 1 oz and at birth a baby weighs only ¹⁄₁₀ oz.

The dwarf lemurs of the genus *Cheirogaleus* are the most squirrel-like lemurs. The rare, hairy-eared dwarf lemur *C. trichotis* lives in the eastern forest; a grey dwarf lemur lives in dry forest, and this is the common fat-tailed lemur *C. medius*. The greater dwarf lemur *C. major* is much larger than the others. Cocquerel's mouse lemur *Microcebus cocquereli* is a rare species and is twice the size of most mouse lemurs. The fork-marked lemur *Phaner furcifer* is 2 ft long and has a black-forked band on its head from which it derives its name. The very small lemurs we have just mentioned can aestivate in hollow tree trunks and sustain themselves through periods of scarcity, thanks to their reserve of fat. This dormant period of torpor takes place during the dry season, hence it is called aestivation and not hibernation.

Lemuroids are the truly characteristic animals of the island. They have nocturnal species, and crepuscular or diurnal, and a somewhat monkey-like appearance. Gentle lemurs are diurnal. Their activity takes place during the day and they have a vegetarian diet. This species lives in small groups. The grey gentle lemur *Hapalemur griseus* eats bamboo shoots and lives in the interior and to the west of the island. The broad-nosed gentle lemur *H. sinus* is contained in the east and lives in the reeds of the shores.

The members of the genus *Lemur* are diurnal and there are six species known, all of which are arboreal (with the exception of the ring-tailed lemur). The ruffed lemur *L. variegatus* has nocturnal habits but can be

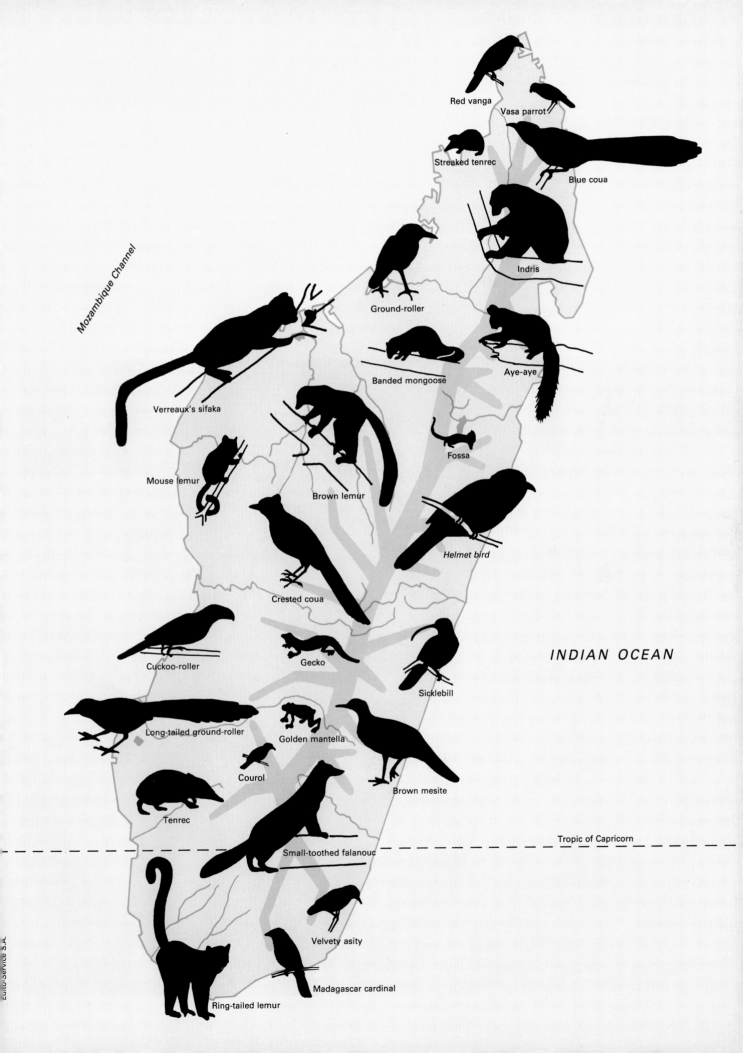

Red vanga

Vasa parrot

Streaked tenrec

Blue coua

Indris

Mozambique Channel

Ground-roller

Banded mongoose

Aye-aye

Verreaux's sifaka

Fossa

Mouse lemur

Brown lemur

Helmet bird

Crested coua

INDIAN OCEAN

Cuckoo-roller

Gecko

Sicklebill

Long-tailed ground-roller

Golden mantella

Brown mesite

Courol

Tenrec

Small-toothed falanouc

Tropic of Capricorn

Velvety asity

Madagascar cardinal

Ring-tailed lemur

seen in the morning. A sub-species of the ring-tailed lemur *L. catta* is an inhabitant of mountainous and barren regions.

Other lemurs include the black lemur *L. macaco*, whose males and females have a different coat, the brown lemur *L. fulvus* and the mongoose lemur *L. mongoz*, which has two races, one in the Comoro Islands, the other in Central Madagascar. Finally, there is the very rare red-bellied lemur *L. rubiventer*. All of these different lemurs have interesting habits and behaviour.

There are two species of the genus *Lepilemur*: the sportive lemur *L. ruficaudatus* and the weasel or playful lemur *L. mustelinus*. These leaf-eating lemurs have upper incisors that fall out when they are still quite young.

Sifakas, indris and aye-ayes

Madagascan species are vanishing as a result of the over-exploitation of the island's for-ests. Though there were once very large lemuroids, notably *Megaladis*, the largest prosimians today are those of the family Indriidae.

The members of this family worth a closer look are the sifakas, the indri and the woolly sifaka. The last is nocturnal, the others diurnal; all are vegetarians. They are characterized by their method of moving–which they do in an upright position through a series of jumps.

The sifakas of the genus *Propithecus* (p. 2253) have a long tail and extensible skin between their upper arm and body. There are two species: the Verreaux sifaka *P. verreauxi* and the diademed sifaka *P. diadema*, of which there are several sub-species. The woolly sifaka *Avahe laniger* has huge eyes and is active at night. The indri *Indri indri* is a larger species, but with a much shorter tail, around 2 in. long–as opposed to the 16 in.

tail of the woolly sifaka. The indri is active during the day and is characterized by its great ears, long hands, and face with its naked muzzle. It is the pre-eminently Madagascan animal, and its upright move-ment leaves a strange impression on the mind.

The aye-aye *Daubentomia madagascariensis* (p. 265) is very special; for a long time naturalists have hesitated to class it with other Madagascan prosimians. It is usually placed in its own family, the Dauben-toniidae. It lives in isolated bamboo jungles of the north where the trees are generously endowed with insect larvae. Today the aye-aye is extremely rare, although protected colonies are breeding.

Other mammals

The small-toothed mongoose or falanouc *Eupleres goudoti* and the greater falanouc *E.*

The ring-tailed lemur lives in groups which fiercely defend their territory against their neighbours.

major, which feed on ants and other insects, are important Madagascan viverrid mammals – even though little is known about them. The island's largest carnivore is the reddish-brown fossa *Cryptoprocta ferox*. It is compared to both the mongoose and civet with which it shares some characteristics. To many it looks like a small, long-headed puma. The Madagascan mongooses (p. 1638) are nocturnal and live in thick forest – which makes them difficult to observe. In the east, the ringed-tailed mongoose *Galidia elegans* is the least known of Madagascan species. But there are four other species: the broad-striped mongoose *G. striata*, the narrow-striped mongoose *Mungotictis substriata*, the banded mongoose *G. fasciata* and the unicoloured mongoose *Salonoia unicolor*. Now the only species of its genus, the Madagascan civet *Fossa fossa* (p. 576) should not be confused with the fossa already mentioned.

A little known creature, this civet eats small mammals and other creatures as well as insects.

One cannot speak of Madagascar without mentioning tenrecs (p. 2497), strange insectivores which are comparable in certain respects to both hedgehogs and shrews – and whose bodies are between 1½ in. and 20 in. long. These are only found on the island and form a group unique in its genus. The tailless tenrec *Tenrec ecaudatus* is the best known species.

There are some 30 species of tenrecs: the streaked tenrec *Hemicentetes semispinosus* resembles a smaller version of the tailless tenrec and is equally at home in humid regions of the shore or rain forests. Hedgehog-tenrecs are of the genera *Setifer* and *Echinops*, and consist of the great hedgehog-tenrec *S. setosus* and the little hedgehog-tenrec *E. telfairi*. In the marshy

regions of Madagascar live the rice and long-tailed tenrecs. The rice tenrecs (*Oryzorictes* spp) are so called as they inhabit the moist banks of rice fields. The long-tailed tenrecs (*Microgale* spp) occur in forested regions and are shrew-like in appearance and habit. The web-footed tenrec *Limnogale mergulus* is an aquatic tenrec with fringed forefeet and webbed toes. Another species of tenrec *Geogale aurita* lives along the west coast and is the least known of the island's fascinating mammals.

Representative birds
The couas of the island are non-parasitic cuckoos that feed on insects and molluscs. The crested coua *Coua cristata* and the blue coua *C. coerulea* are quite beautiful and most colourful, compared to the dull plumage of most cuckoos. According to some ornithologists, the ten Madagascan couas belong to

The diet of all tenrecs consists of small invertebrates. They also seem to eat more plant food than true hedgehogs.

The Madagascan cardinal Foudia madagascariensis. *Only the male has the brilliant scarlet plumage. The female is a dull fawn-brown colour.*

the same sub-family as the coucals (p. 674), which they greatly resemble. Each continent, except for Australia, has its groups of non-parasitic cuckoos, but couas of the sub-family Couinae only live in Madagascar.

One extremely interesting bird here is the Madagascar cardinal *Foudia madagascariensis*, which is also known as the fodi. This finch-like bird owes its name of cardinal to the male's scarlet plumage.

Three exclusively Madagascan families of birds are the Philepittidae, the Vangidae and the Mesitornithidae–which are all pas-serines. Vanga shrikes (p. 2630) have under-gone a special evolution in Madagascar due to their isolation here, and there are a dozen species which can be related to shrikes, especially the wood or helmet shrikes of Africa, which they resemble considerably. The Prevost vanga is a sort of miniature

toucan. The sickle-beaked vanga has a wail-ing cry and, as a result, the natives call it a baby-bird. The helmetbird *Euryceros prevosti* and sicklebill or falcula *Falculea palliata* are members of the same family, the Vangidae (though for some reason they are often mentioned apart). Vanga shrikes are so diversified, in fact, that they constitute a sort of natural laboratory for the study of evol-ution. The Madagascan nuthatch *Hypositta corallirostris* and a bulbul, *Tylas eduardi*, are also part of this family.

The velvety asity or philepitta *Philepitta castanea* is a Madagascan relic species of bird, small, plump and long-legged, looking rather like a South American pitta. The cuckoo-roller *Leptosomus discolor* is another survivor of a prehistoric past and quite large at 16½ in.

Madagascar has three species of mesites (p. 1591), which are placed among the order

Gruiformes along with rails, and these birds are regarded as sacred. The brown mesite *Mesoenas unicolor* is rare, and lives in the rain forest of the east coast; the white-breasted mesite *M. variegata* inhabits the dry forest of the north and south-west. Mesites live on the ground; their wings are normally developed, but they have weak collar bones and cannot do much more than flutter.

Small-sized parrots, the grey-headed love-bird *Agapornis cana* (p. 1480) and the great black parrot *Coracopsis vasa* are everywhere on the island. The first of them colonizes rice plantations. Multi-coloured birds are rep-resented by rollers (p. 2112) of the family Coraciadidae. The cuckoo-roller, already mentioned, is of a closely related sub-family. Ground rollers of the family Brachyp-teraciidae are an intermediary group en-demic to the island, and distinct from true rollers although some zoologists think they are aberrant members of the roller family. There are five species in three genera: *Uratelornis*, *Atelornis* and *Brachypteracias*. The long-tailed ground roller *U. chimaera* has a long tail and powerful claws and lives in the sub-desert bush country of the south-west. The pitta-like ground roller *A. pittoides* and its cousin *A. crossleyi*, the short-legged ground roller *B. leptosomus* are all birds of the dense forest; they live there on the ground in heavy damp thickets.

Nocturnal birds of prey are considerably more numerous on the island than diurnal ones. The black or pariah kite *Milvus migrans* (p. 1372) is a good example of the latter group.

Close to the water one encounters the original comb or knob-billed duck *Sarkidiornis melanotos*; some tree ducks like the widowed tree duck *Dendrocygna viduata* (p. 2559); the Madagascan teal *Anas bernieri* (p. 2492), also called royal bird; and the pygmy goose *Nettapus auritus*—which has beautiful feathers which mingle in a harmony of primary colours.

Drongos (p. 806) and fly-catchers (p. 943) are birds of steppes, plains and wooded steppes. Drongos have adapted in typical ways to catch insects—though the seven species of Africa and Madagascar are the most primitive and have few refinements. The genus *Dicrurus* is well distributed throughout the islands. Fly-catchers are a great heterogenous group. In the Old World there are fly-catchers of the family Muscicapidae; in the New World, Tyrannidae. All of them insect-eaters, fly-catchers vary considerably in appearance (especially when one takes intermediary forms into consideration). Madagascan tit-babblers (p. 266) are a sub-family of the babbling thrushes. They are small, short-winged, often colourful birds with strong legs that live mainly in thickets, grass and reeds.

Reptiles and amphibians

As we have said, there are no venomous reptiles on the island. The Madagascan constrictor *Acrantophis madagascariensis* and the boa *Sanzinia madagascariensis* are very similar to South American boas and constrictors. One strange snake of the genus *Lioheterodon* lives on the ground and has an upturned snout remarkably like the hog-nosed snakes of America. Another special reptile, the Madagascan rear-fanged snake *Langaha nasuta* has a long appendage on its snout and feeds on tree frogs and birds.

Day geckos (p. 1008) of the genus *Phelsuma* are prominent in Madagascar and the neighbouring archipelagos. These handsome bright green geckos with their bodies splashed with red spots are active during the day and can be mimetic according to habitat. The best known is the Madagascan day gecko *P. madagascariensis*. But the family also includes the four-eyed day gecko *P. quadriocellata*, which lives in the centre and to the

The comb duck Sarkidiornis melanotos, *also known as the knob-billed goose.*

The chameleon's feet are adapted for moving in the trees. All chameleons have the ability to change colour.

south of the island. The leaf-tailed gecko *Uroplatus fimbriatus* is active at night. This Madagascan resident is a really strange creature. Its body is flat, and its skin is exactly like bark, with the sides of the body and limbs having peculiarly fringed scales (as its common name suggests). As a result it is perfectly camouflaged. No-one knows the purpose of the scales with which it is covered, but this creature can change colour according to moods or the place it wishes to merge with.

Iguanas (p. 1296) are adapted to the most varied habitats – to the point that the lifestyle of one species is sometimes quite different from that of another, even though they may resemble each other closely in appearance. Iguanas are found in both North and South America, Fiji and Tonga, as well as Madagascar. The agama lizards (p. 59) live in Europe, Africa, Asia and Australia – where 'flying dragons' are found.

By the beginning of the Tertiary period, the better adapted agamids had already pushed out the iguana. But true agamas

never managed to reach Madagascar. Iguanas had a very widespread distribution in ancient times – which their presence on the island tends to prove, even if only two kinds are left. Six of the seven species of Madagascan iguanas are of the genus *Hoplurus*. They are rock or semi-arboreal lizards with spiny tails and very strongly keeled scales. The other iguana is the smooth-scaled iguana *Chalarodon madagascariensis*. It is a slender and agile, essentially terrestrial, creature with a preference for sandy soil. It has a distinctive crest of large scales.

The small golden mantella *Mantella aurentiaca*, about 1 in. long, lives in wet forests on the island. It is fertilized internally and the female produces its eggs without the participation of the male. It was once thought to be related to the tropical American arrow-poison frogs (Dendrobatidae).

Chameleons (p. 546) are considered descendants of the agama, and quite apart from their innate strangeness, very little is known about their natural behaviour. There are a great number of Madagascan cha-

meleons. The giant Madagascan chameleon *(Chamaeleo oustaleti)* can grow to 25 in. long and have a 14 in. tail. This very large lizard eats young mice when in captivity. The warted chameleon *C. verrucosus*, which belongs to the same family, is a little smaller, lives in dry forests and can tolerate high temperatures. The panther chameleon *C. pardalis* is found in dense and humid forests. Parson's chameleon *C. parsonii* has two horn-shaped growths on its snout. The male short-horned chameleon *C. brevicornis* has large flattened scales on its snout, which the female lacks. *Chamaeleo lateralis*, which is normally green, changes colour dramatically when excited. Another 'horned' chameleon is the fork-nosed chameleon *C. furcifer*.

Stump-tailed chameleons of the genus *Brookesia* are found on the island and have many special features. One species is the brookesia with jutting eyebrows *Brookesia supercilarius*. The smallest species (*B. tuberculata*) which is barely more than 1 in. long, lives in a northern zone. Finally, the horned or armoured chameleon *Leandria perarmata*,

4–5 in. long, carries a double row of spines on its back and tail. In general, the chameleons have prehensile tails, but the stump-tailed chameleons can only curl up the tip of their short tails and cannot coil them round a twig. Each species displays great varieties of coloration, but the mood of the animal is the principal factor in its changes of colour. Chameleons are tree-dwellers but can make do with bushes. Stump-tailed species even exist on the forest floor and live happily in regions where there is little vegetation.

Tortoises (p. 2550) constitute almost a world in themselves: with 66 genera and about 220 species, living mainly in warmer regions of the world. They divide initially into two sub-orders, the hidden-necked turtles and tortoises, the Cryptodia, and the side-necked turtles of the order Pleurodira.

One of the smallest of land tortoises *Pyxis arachnoides*–which has a 4-in. shell or carapace with a spider-web pattern–lives on the island. The tortoises of the principal genus *Testudo*, are represented by the rayed or starred tortoise of Madagascar *T. radiata*.

△ *Parson's chameleon* Chamaeleo parsonii, *one of the many Madagascan chameleons.*

▽ *Hidden-necked turtles bend their necks horizontally when they retreat into their shells.*

Flying foxes of the genus Pteropus *hanging from the trees.*

Southern Africa has at least three species of *Testudo*. The giant tortoise *T. gigantea* once lived in the Comores, where it has been exterminated. But Madagascar still has enormous specimens. Leatherback sea turtles, like the giant leatherback *Dermochelys coriacea* (p. 1423), have a carapace of nearly 6 ft long which weighs 1300 lb. These are the largest turtles in the world.

Madagascar has two species of hidden-necked turtles (p. 1202) of the family Pelomedusidae. One rarity is the river turtle *Podocnemis madagascariensis*. The other river turtles of this genus are South American, and once again Madagascar shows how animal distribution was once very different from that which exists today.

Bats

Bats are the only mammals truly capable of flying. They sub-divide into fruit-eating bats (Megachiroptera) and insect-eating bats (Microchiroptera). Megachiroptera are only found in the Old World and chiefly in tropical humid forests. Microchiroptera are well represented in the New World and one family, the Phyllostomatidae, has fruit-eating species. (One African species only eats nectar.)

Madagascar has some distinct species of its own. The giant flying fox *Pteropus giganteus* (p. 947) which is distributed widely through Asia and Australasia, is also quite numerous on the island, as is the red flying fox *P. rufus*. Madagascar is the home of the sole species of

the family Myzopodidae. This is the sucker-footed bat *Myzopoda aurita*, which has adhesive discs on its wrists and ankles, which probably allow it to fasten itself on to the hard stems and leaves of palms and other smooth surfaces.

Butterflies and moths

Finally, Madagascar has some beautiful butterflies and moths like the great comet *Argema mittrei* which is 8 in. long with a 7-in. wing span. The comet is one of the largest butterflies known, but the island also provides a home for the perhaps even lovelier jewel of Madagascar, the urania moth *Chrysiridia madagascarensis*. Although renowned for its beauty, little is known of this moth's habits.

Magpie

This bird, a member of the crow family, was originally called a pie; the feminine prefix Mag was added at about the end of the 16th century. At a distance the magpie looks black and white but seen close to, especially when the sun is shining on it, its plumage is shot with iridescent blue and green. The magpie is 18 in. long, of which 10 in. is tail. It is known in North America as the black-billed magpie, to distinguish it from a slightly smaller bird otherwise like it except for its yellow bill. The yellow-billed magpie is found in the farming areas of California. The azure-winged magpie found in Portugal and parts of Spain, eastern China and Japan is 13 in. long with a black cap, light brown back, white front and blue wings and tail. Even more colourful is the green magpie of southeast Asia, from the Himalayas to Sumatra and Borneo. It is a light green with darker green on wings and tail, an orange bill, black eye-stripe and brown and black on the wings. The Ceylon blue magpie is a rich blue with brown head and shoulders and brown flight feathers.

Thieving magpies

The common magpie is an eye-catching bird with its long tail and relatively short wings and its chattering cries. It lives in woods, parkland or well-wooded farmland. Usually it is seen in ones, twos or threes, but may form small flocks in winter or when going to roost. When it lands the long tail is at once held up and carried clear of the ground. It usually walks although it may hop sideways with slightly opened wings to inspect food or a bright object. It will readily take bright objects and hide them—the 'thieving magpie' is proverbial.

No food refused

Although the magpie's food is mainly insects there seems no limit to what it will take, from small invertebrates such as snails, slugs and worms, to young rabbits, rats and mice. It is a notorious egg-stealer and will also take nestlings and fledglings of songbirds. It has been known to attack sickly or injured livestock and there is a record of a group of magpies, in hard weather, attacking the wounds of a saddle-sore donkey, eventually killing it, then eating the carrion. The magpie is one of the few birds in the British Isles known to attack and kill adders. Where game birds are preserved the magpie is shot on sight. Nevertheless, elsewhere than in game preserves, magpies have been found, on balance, to be beneficial to agri-

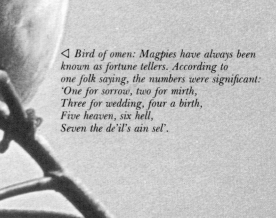

◁ Bird of omen: Magpies have always been known as fortune tellers. According to one folk saying, the numbers were significant:
'One for sorrow, two for mirth,
Three for wedding, four a birth,
Five heaven, six hell,
Seven the de'il's ain sel'.

culture because of the insects they take. They will often perch on cattle, sheep and deer to clean up the ticks. Plant food is also eaten, especially grain, acorns, nuts, beech-mast, berries, peas, potatoes and fruits.

Roof of thorns
Breeding begins in April, both partners of a pair combining to build a large nest in a tall tree, thorn bush or overgrown hedge, or sometimes on telephone poles. The nest is made of sticks cemented with mud and lined with fine roots, dry grass or hair. Typically a domed roof of thorny twigs covers the nest, but this may sometimes be missing. Usually 5 or 6, rarely up to 10, greenish-blue or yellow-ish eggs, spotted and mottled with brown or grey, are laid and incubated by the female alone, for 17–18 days. The nestlings are fed by both parents for about a month. Young magpies have the pied plumage of the parents, but they have short tails.

Ceremonial assemblies
Magpies are sometimes seen in spring in larger groups than usual, from half a dozen to as many as 200, in what are called cere-monial assemblies. The meaning of these assemblies is not clear but the air of excite-ment about them is always obvious. They may have something to do with breeding since the birds seem to be moving about in pairs within the group. They hop about on the branches of trees or on the ground, or take slow flights into the air. They chase each other, posture and raise and lower their head feathers and raise the tail, open-ing and closing it like a fan. These assemblies may be purely social, since they sometimes take place outside the breeding season.

No enemies?
Magpies may sometimes be killed by the larger birds of prey, or by ground predators such as foxes. It is highly unlikely that they suffer serious losses since they are so agile and able to defend themselves.

Valiant brigands
Of the magpie's total length of 1½ ft nearly half is tail, and it weighs half a pound al-though its body is not much bigger than that of a blackbird which weighs half this. The difference in weight between the two birds is largely accounted for by the mag-pie's large head, powerful beak and strong legs and toes. In addition to the beak and toes a magpie has speed and manoeuvra-bility in attack. Above all, its fighting tactics are superb. A magpie comes in to attack and as it is warded off it retreats with a semi-hovering flight, flying backwards to just out of reach but still facing the enemy and ready to come in swiftly once more. A mag-pie, small in body, can make a quick stab, retreat and return for rapid strikes.

Magpies often hop over the ground and, when excited, do so while flicking their wings half-open and closing them again. When fighting, and therefore excited, they also flick their wings which now give lift to the hopping so the birds cover the ground in airborne hops of up to 2 ft each. Two mag-pies attacking from ground level, using the half-hovering thrust and retreat and the half-flying hop, seem like half a dozen birds.

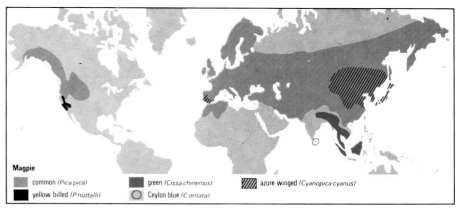

Magpie
- common *(Pica pica)*
- yellow-billed *(P. nuttalli)*
- green *(Cissa chinensis)*
- Ceylon blue *(C. ornata)*
- azure-winged *(Cyanopica cyanus)*

Arthur Christiansen

AF Taylor

class	**Aves**
order	**Passeriformes**
family	**Corvidae**
genera & species	*Cissa chinensis* green magpie *C. ornata* Ceylon blue magpie *Cyanopica cyanus* azure-winged magpie *Pica nuttalli* yellow-billed magpie *P. pica* common magpie

△ △ *Tell-tail story. The wing imprints at the side of the long, broken line show the path of an excited magpie hopping over the snow-covered ground, flapping its wings with each jerky bound.*
△ *Winter garden party. A group of magpies gather round a rabbit they have found. Magpies sometimes collect round carrion in winter when food is scarce.*

Magpie-lark

The two magpie-larks belong to a family of birds, appropriately known as 'mudnest-builders', that live in Australia and New Guinea. The magpie-lark, mudlark, or peewit of Australia is the size of a European blackbird or American robin, and is neither a magpie nor a lark. Its plumage is black and white, being mainly black on the back, head and breast and with a black tip to the tail. The females differ in lacking a white 'eyebrow' and in having a white throat.

The mudlark is found in many parts of Australia while its smaller relative is confined to the mountains of New Guinea. Also in the family of 'mudnest-builders' are the Australian apostlebird and white-winged chough. The former is larger than the magpie-lark and has grey plumage. The name apostlebird is derived from its habit of associating in flocks of about 12 birds. The white-winged chough, no relation of true choughs (p. 568), is the largest in the family. It is 18 in. long with glossy black plumage and a white patch on each wing.

Eccentric fliers

Magpie-larks live in open countryside and have adapted themselves to life in suburbs, where their abundance and flashy plumage has made them very popular. They mate for life and a pair keeps the same territory from year to year, but in the winter some adults join flocks of immature magpie-larks numbering several hundreds—sometimes thousands. Magpie-larks in a flock roost together, often on the same site year after year. They also display communally in spectacular feats of flying, which are seen most often when they leave the roost. They fly wildly through the trees in a mad rush, twisting and turning and sometimes brushing the foliage with their wings. Another habit is for the flock to soar around in circles, weaving in and out, landing, then repeating the manoeuvre.

Farmer's friend

Magpie-larks feed on pastures, swamps and on the banks of rivers where they find insects, such as locusts and flies, and other invertebrates, such as worms. They are beneficial because they eat insect pests such as cutworms and grasshoppers, and the snails which carry flukes (p. 939) that infest stock. The opening up of the country has favoured the magpie-larks as it has provided them with large supplies of insect food. Dung is searched for grubs, and stable flies are caught as they emerge, before their wings have dried and they can escape. In northern Australia magpie-larks are called 'stock-inspectors' because they perch on the backs of domestic animals and remove the ticks from their skin.

Mud castles

At the start of the breeding season, male magpie-larks advertise for mates with calls

▷ *Half-way rest house. Two young magpie-larks pause before they come to the ground to feed.*

Popperfoto

of 'pee-o-wit' which give them one of their popular names. Several males may compete for one female but once she has been attracted to one male the pair leave to set up a territory of 15–20 acres. They sing duets, one bird calling 'pee-o-wit' and the other immediately answering 'te-he'. The territory is defended against other magpie-larks, each bird attacking intruders of its own sex. Passing birds of prey are also noisily attacked.

Magpie-larks begin breeding at the onset of the rains and nest near lakes or rivers. It seems that open water is a necessary stimulus for nesting, which is not surprising as much mud is needed for the nest, and in dry years magpie-larks may fail to breed. The nest is like an earthenware bowl placed on the branch of a tree. The mud is carefully collected and moulded with the breast to form a bowl 6 in. across and 3 in. deep with walls $\frac{3}{4}$ in. thick. The walls are strengthened by the inclusion of grass, feathers and horsehair, but broods are sometimes lost when the nest is washed away by rain. Butcherbirds (p. 467) also cause losses by driving away the magpie-larks and raiding nests.

Both parents incubate the 2–5 eggs which are white with violet patches. The chicks are fed by both parents and they stay in the nest for 2–3 weeks, then perch in the treetops before coming to the ground to feed themselves. Later the young birds form flocks and the parents raise a second brood, providing there is still open water nearby. When breeding has finished the parents may join the flocks of immature birds.

Sharing nests

The apostlebirds and white-winged choughs also make nests of mud and they nest communally. The choughs live in small flocks of up to 20 birds and all help to build the nest, incubate the eggs and feed the young. Only a few of the females, however, lay eggs, for one nest contains only 2–8 eggs. Moreover, perhaps only two chicks survive to leave the nest. The eggs usually hatch out but the desire of several parents or foster parents to brood the chicks leads to most of them being trampled upon or smothered. This seems to be a most inefficient means of breeding, in which only a few females lay and many chicks die before fledging, but the habits of the white-winged choughs are not well known, and it may prove that there is some advantage in this behaviour, or that it only occurs at certain times when it is desirable to limit the number of young.

class	**Aves**
order	**Passeriformes**
family	**Grallinidae**
genera & species	***Corcorax melanorhamphos*** *white-winged chough* ***Grallina bruijni*** *New Guinea magpie-lark* ***G. cyanoleuca*** *Australian magpie-lark* ***Struthidea cinerea*** *apostlebird*

▷ *Out on a limb. The mud-cemented, bowl-shaped nest of the Australian magpie-lark is built on the branch of a tree.*

Maize moth

The maize moth is a native of Europe but has been introduced to North America, where it is called the corn-borer. The American name is more commonly used because it is in the United States that the moth has become a terrible pest of corn, or maize as it is called in Europe.

The adult maize moth is a small moth with a wingspread of 1 in. The female is yellowish-brown with dark wavy lines running irregularly across the wings. The male is very much darker than this with markings of olive brown. Maize moths are nocturnal and fly strongly.

Explosive spread

Maize moths live in Europe and Asia. The larvae have been found on about 200 kinds of plants, including maize, beet, celery, beans and garden flowers. In England they have been found on mugwort and hops. Maize moths lived in Europe for many thousands of years before maize was introduced from America in the 16th century, but maize became a favoured food plant because it fulfilled the larvae's nutritional requirements and also provided them with shelter all the year round. As a result, when they were accidentally taken to North America they very rapidly colonised the extensive crops of maize.

It is thought that the first to reach North America may have arrived about 1907, in cargoes of maize from Hungary or Italy. The first positive discovery of these moths in the United States came, however, in 1917 when crops near Boston were found to be infected. Two years after this the maize moth appeared around the Great Lakes, and by then it had become so well established that large-scale programmes of eradication failed and the insect eventually reached the Midwest cornbelt.

Today it is a major pest in the United States and occasionally whole crops of maize are ruined because the larvae so weaken the stems by burrowing that the plants topple over. If modern insecticides had been available in 1917 the insect would probably have been checked. Compulsory burning of the remains of maize plants and weeds after harvesting proved an unsatisfactory method of control.

By 1920 about 100 species of insect pests had been introduced into the United States, although this number has now been reduced by careful controls. The ease with which introduced insects flourish in the United States is due to the absence of enemies and diseases of the insects that kept their numbers within bounds in their original homes.

Caterpillars like to be snug

The eggs of the maize moth are laid on the undersides of leaves in groups of 5–50, each female laying 600 or more. They hatch in about a week. The caterpillars are flesh-coloured with small brown spots. They feed until half-grown in spaces between the ears or leaves of the maize and the stalks. Then they eat into the stalks and ears, making tunnels through the tissues until they are

△ *Female maize moth lays a mass of 20–30 eggs.*
▽ *Pupa of the European corn borer (× 6).*

▽ *Working its way to the top. Another maize stalk borer* **Busseola fusca** *from Africa (× 4).*

fully grown, at ¾–1 in. long. There is usually no more than one caterpillar on each plant, but when there is a heavy infestation the maize plants in a field may have about ten caterpillars each. Even so mortality is high before they enter the plant. Heavy rain causes many deaths of emerging caterpillars, and if the summer is very dry they perish before they can bore into plants.

The caterpillars spend winter in their tunnels then pupate the next spring and hatch out in summer.

Maize the perfect host

If an animal is a pest it becomes the focus of scientific studies. These studies may seem to bear little relation to the destructive habits of the animal, but it is important to investigate every facet of the animal's life to find out, first why it is a pest, and secondly, the weak links in its life cycle which can be attacked by control methods.

One essential problem in the study of the maize moth was why it preferred maize to other plants. One reason, it was found, was that the life cycle of maize fits in well with the life cycle of the moth. Maize is planted in early spring and the leaves are sprouting just in time for the moths to lay their eggs. The leaves provide a steady source of food through the year and in winter the dead stalks provide a very necessary shelter for the resting caterpillars.

Closer examination showed that the caterpillars prefer some parts of the plant more than others. At first they feed in the tightly rolled whorl of leaves wrapped around the stalk. When the flower head develops they feed there. As the flowers expand, the caterpillars move back into the leaf bases and into the husks surrounding the ears. Tests showed that this movement was due to the caterpillar's dislike of light and preference for being in crevices with as much of the body as possible against something solid.

Even within these preferred snug parts of the maize plant, the maize moths still exercised preferences. They move to flowers rather than leaves, to inner husks rather than outer husks because these parts contain more sugar. An unusual reason was found for the liking for sugar. Young maize plants contain a chemical poisonous to maize moths, and sugar acts as an antidote. The chemical is the maize plant's natural remedy against maize moths and some of them are killed by it, but the ones that can eat a sufficient amount of sugar are safe.

These facts about the relations of plants and insect pests are not only of interest for their own sake. Once the preferences of the insects are known, it may be possible to breed maize plants in which the pests find it more difficult to survive.

phylum	**Arthropoda**
class	**Insecta**
order	**Lepidoptera**
family	**Pyralididae**
genus & species	***Pyrausta nubilalis***

Mallard

Although there are many species of wild duck the mallard is the one that most people think of as the 'wild duck'. It is the ancestor of most of the domesticated ducks. It is about 2 ft long and weighs 2½ lb. The male, or drake, is brightly coloured from September to June. His belly and most of his back are grey. His head and neck are a dark glossy green and a white ring at the base of the neck separates the green from the brown of the breast. He has small curled feathers on the tail and his voice is a low hoarse call. The female, or duck, is a mottled brown, her voice is a loud quack and she has no curly tail feathers. From July to August the drake is in eclipse plumage, and is unable to fly. That is, he moults his colourful feathers at the end of June, is clothed in a mottling similar to that of the duck, and resumes his coloured plumage at the end of August. Both sexes have wing patches (specula), which are dark or purplish-blue with white edges.

Mallard breed in Europe and Asia from the Arctic Circle southwards to the Mediterranean, Persia, Tibet and Central China, and in northern and central North America. Throughout the range there is a movement south in autumn to Africa, southern Asia and, in America, to Mexico and Florida.

Fritz Siedel

△ *Even waterfowl have to wash — a mallard bathes itself in a shower of spray.*

Make your own duck pond

Wild duck are attracted to any water: from a small pond in woodland to large lakes, to rivers, streams and marshes, although they often live on dry land well away from water. This habit is taken advantage of by wild-fowlers and bird-lovers alike as they can be encouraged to breed quite easily by digging a pond with small islands or floating basket nests. Mallard spend much time on land even when water is available, but whether on water or on land, and apart from feeding, they do little more than stand or sit about, preening from time to time. Indeed, ducks spend a large part of their time simply doing nothing. On land they waddle apparently awkwardly; on water they swim easily and dive only when alarmed. In the air they fly with rapid wingbeats and with neck outstretched, taking off in a steep ascent.

Wide choice of food

Mallard feed by day or by night, mainly on leaves and seeds, grain, berries, acorns, as well as much small animal life such as insects and their larvae, worms, tadpoles, frogs' spawn, small frogs and small fishes. They dabble in mud on land and at the edge of water and upend in deeper water to feed from the mud at the bottom.

▽ *Tired of just dabbling in things, a pair of mallard take to deeper water. The male will lose his lovely plumage once the breeding season is over.*

Arthur Christiansen

Fritz Siedel

△ *Graceless angel about to land, spreads her wings and tail feathers to act as a brake.*

over the heel of the wing making a rattling sound. In shaking the drake draws his head back between his shoulders so the white ring disappears. The feathers on the underside of the body are fluffed out, so the drake appears to ride high on the water. The head feathers are raised so the green sheen disappears and the head rises high so he is almost sitting on his tail on the water, and then he shakes his head up and down.

When a drake grunt-whistles he thrusts his bill almost vertically into the water then throws his head back, scattering a shower of water drops, and as he does this he grunts. Head-up-tail-up is fully descriptive of the next movement, and in the up-and-down movement the bill is quickly thrust into the water and jerked up again with the breast held low in the water. Another movement is known as gasping; one drake utters a low whistle and the rest give a kind of grunt.

These actions may be made in sequence by a group of drakes facing into the centre or by one or two drakes, or between drake and duck. Also, one or other may be seen as isolated actions. Together they form a ritual pattern of courtship carried out in the autumn but actual mating does not take place until spring. More remarkable, in spite of the complicated courtship, there is a high degree of promiscuity in mallard; a drake will mate with a duck while the drake with whom she is paired looks on.

Ritual courtship

Mallard form pairs in autumn and begin breeding in spring. Pairing is preceded by a ritualized courtship. This is initiated by a duck swimming rapidly among a group of drakes with an action that has been called nod-swimming or coquette-swimming. She swims with the neck outstretched and just above water and head nodding. This makes the drakes come together in a tighter group and they begin their communal displays. These are made up of stereotyped actions known as mock drinking, false preening, shaking, grunt-whistling, head-up-tail-up and up-and-down movements. These same movements are seen more easily when the drake and duck are courting.

The duck chooses a drake, who follows her away from the group. She symbolically looks back by turning her head, inciting him to drive away other drakes that may be following. The 'inciting' has become ritualized and is carried out even if no other drakes are there. Mock drinking is a formalized gesture of peace and two drakes meeting head on will 'pretend' to drink. It is a sign they have no intention of attacking each other. In false preening a drake lifts one wing slightly, reaches behind it with his bill as if to preen. Instead, he rubs the bill

High-diving ducklings

The nest, built by the duck, is a shallow saucer of grass, dry leaves and feathers lined with down. It may be on the ground, usually under cover of bushes or in a pol-

▽ *Chicks ahoy! These obedient children always follow when their mother calls them to water very soon after they have dried out from hatching.*

Stephen Dalton: NHPA

Photos: GW Wood

△ *Popping the egg: a duck's first moments of motherhood caught by the camera of reader GW Wood of Eastleigh, Hampshire.*

larded willow, in the disused nest of a large bird such as a crow, or in a hollow in a tree up to 40 ft from the ground. Up to 16, usually 10–12, greyish, green or greenish-buff eggs are laid, from March to October, incubated by the duck alone, for 22–28 days. When the ducklings have dried, soon after hatching, the duck calls them off the nest and leads them to water, or if far from water to a feeding ground. Sometimes the drake is in attendance but takes no part in the care of the ducklings. Even when the nest is 40 ft up in a hollow tree the ducklings leave the nest when the duck calls, each in turn tumbling to the ground without injury. The ducklings are covered with yellowish down broken with large patches of brown. They take nearly 2 months to fledge.

Mother is one enemy

The natural enemies of mallard are birds of prey and ground predators such as foxes. These probably have little effect on mallard populations. The main losses are at the duckling stage. A duck may hatch a brood of 12 and in a fortnight be left with only one duckling. Crows, rooks, magpies, rats and other ducks attack the ducklings. The duck herself may tread on one or more or sit on them in the water, drowning one or two. By contrast, the same duck may then lay a second clutch of 12 and rear all the ducklings to fledging.

Moby duck

When a duck dabbles its bill in mud it is doing much the same as when a large whalebone whale opens its huge mouth and swims through a mass of krill. Both are using a highly efficient filter in which transverse plates on the inner edges of the duck's bill play the part of the baleen plates of the whale. As the duck dabbles its tongue acts as a piston sucking water or mud into the mouth and driving it out again. Only the edible particles are left behind on the transverse plates, but how the sorting out is done nobody knows. It used to be thought birds had no taste buds, the groups of cells on the tongue that give a sense of taste. Mallard have, however, 200 arranged in rows along the sides of the tongue. It may be these that tell the duck how to sort out edible from inedible particles.

class	**Aves**
order	**Anseriformes**
family	**Anatidae**
genus & species	***Anas platyrhynchus***

◁ *Centre of attention. A coquette-swimming female is displayed to by one of the drakes performing his exhibitionist grunt-whistle.*
▽ *Up tails all! Mallard often feed upside down in deeper water.*

Photos: Jane Burton · Photo Res

Mallee fowl

The mallee fowl belongs to a group of birds which do not use their own body heat to hatch their eggs. In this they resemble reptiles, but use more refined methods than any egg-laying reptiles. The mallee fowl is one of a family of a dozen species of turkey-like birds living in the Indo-Australian region, known variously as megapodes (big feet), scrubfowl, brush-turkeys, mound-builders and incubator birds. In Australia some of them are spoken of as jungle fowl. Of these, the mallee fowl has been the most completely studied and has the most astonishing nesting habits.

The plumage of megapodes is mainly brown or mottled browns and greys with some colouring on neck and breast. This may be slate grey to red although some species have a bare neck. In the mallee fowl the front of the neck and the breast is decorated with a line of tufts of dark feathers. The tail is usually long and shaped like that of a turkey. The legs and toes are large and strong. Megapodes, like pheasants and related gamebirds, feed on seeds and leaves as well as insects and other small invertebrates, largely found by scratching the ground.

The distribution of the family is from the Nicobar islands in the Indian Ocean eastwards through the Malay Archipelago to the Philippines and Polynesia, and southwards to Australia. The habitat ranges from tropical rain forest to semi-dry scrub. The mallee fowl itself is found among the dry scrub of inland Australia, where water is scarce and the bird can go without drinking if necessary.

Automatic incubation

Mallee fowl and other megapodes do not brood their eggs like other birds, they incubate them by the heat of the sun, volcanic steam or even huge compost heaps. Some megapodes merely scratch out a pit in the sand, lay their eggs in this and cover them with sand, leaving them to be incubated by the heat of the surrounding ground. On islands, in the Solomons and elsewhere, certain megapodes scratch pits where volcanic steam finds its way through the soil, and the heat from this incubates the eggs. Other species simply lay their eggs in cracks in sunheated rocks. It is in dense jungles that mound-building reaches its height. There, several pairs of birds build mounds of sand or dead leaves, in varying proportions, up to 35 ft in diameter and 15 ft high. The females dig tunnels into the mound and lay their eggs. The brush turkeys build smaller mounds, 12 ft in diameter and 3 ft high, in warm moist jungles, where the pile of leaves ferments rapidly and generates much heat. The male tests the mound regularly with his beak, turning the rotting leaves over and mixing them until the correct temperature is reached. Then he allows the hen to lay in the mound before taking charge again.

△ *All in a flap. Two mallee fowl fluffing and flustering in display.*

John Warham

Incubation in a compost heap

How the brush turkey works is not known but it may be in a similar way to the mallee fowl, which has been exhaustively studied by the Australian scientist HJ Frith. Mallee fowl do not reach maturity until 3 years old. Then they pair up and dig a huge pit in the dry sand. There is so little vegetation where they live that they must rake into the pit all the vegetable litter over a radius of 50 yd. They do this in June, which is the beginning of the southern winter. Then the rains come, soaking the heap of litter. It begins to heat up with the bacterial action of rotting, and in August the birds begin to mix sand with the vegetable rubbish in a pit at the centre of the mound, to form an incubation chamber. Egg-laying begins in September, by which time the temperature in the incubation chamber should have reached 33°C/92°F. The male tests it with his open beak, the tongue presumably acting as his thermometer, and if the temperature is right he allows the hen to lay. She also tests the temperature and if satisfied scrapes away a small part of the mixture of sand and leaf and lays her first egg in the hole, broad end uppermost. The male replaces the mixture to cover in the incubation chamber, then rakes the rest of the vegetable matter over the top to make the mound complete once more. This is repeated at irregular intervals throughout the next 4 months, the hen laying another egg at intervals of 2 days or more, sometimes as much as 17 days after the last egg. The male throughout inspects the nest daily to make sure the temperature is correct. The number of eggs laid may be anything up to 33, each 4 in. long and weighing nearly

Graham Pizzey: Photo Res

◁ *Straight from the oven! A young mallee fowl pushes its way out of its incubation chamber for its first breath of fresh air.*

▽ *Earthworks. A male mallee fowl, after excavating the mound, descends the pit to check the heating system below, and if necessary, adjust it.*

Graham Pizzey: Photo Res

△ *A mallee fowl's home is his castle: strong legs splayed for grip on the sand, a mallee fowl stands atop the results of his labours.*

E Slater

½ lb. The hen herself weighs only 3½ lb, so she lays about 4 times her own weight of eggs in a season.

Herculean labours

The temperature of the air varies throughout each day and night and also changes with the seasons. To keep it steady inside the mound means moving and replacing huge amounts of leaves and rubbish every time there is a rise or fall in its temperature. If the mound becomes too hot the male opens it up at the top to let the heat out. Sh—. 'd the mound show signs of getting too cool it is opened up still more to let the sun's rays fall directly on the incubation chamber, the material removed being spread beyond the rim of the crater so it can absorb as much heat as possible from the sun. So it goes on, the male repeatedly testing the temperature and taking the necessary steps to correct it. He may even at times have to throw a layer of soil onto the mound to hold in the heat.

No help for the chicks

As soon as the last egg is laid the first will be hatching. The chicks find their own way to the surface. On arrival there they push their heads out to breathe and rest for a while. Then they heave their bodies out and totter to the nearest shade to rest for a day before starting to look for food. Some die in trying to get out, especially when the mound has been covered with a layer of soil and this has baked hard.

Ninety per cent hatching

Mallee fowl have no natural enemies except introduced foxes. Frith watched over 70 mallee mounds containing a total of 1 094 eggs. Of these 15 were broken, 130 failed to hatch and 407 were eaten by foxes. This means that but for the foxes there would be 90% hatching of chicks and this with the large clutches suggests a heavy mortality in each generation. Either there used to be natural enemies, perhaps thylacines or others, before foxes were introduced, or, which is more likely, many mallee fowl die each year because there is so little food for them in the desert.

Centuries' old riddle

In 1519 Magellan set out to circumnavigate the globe. The expedition met disaster and Magellan himself never returned. One of the survivors was Gemelli Careri and in his memoirs, written after his return in 1522, he spoke of a bird about the size of a small fowl that laid eggs bigger than itself and buried them in the ground to be hatched by the heat from the sun and sand. HJ Frith, who has studied the mallee fowl, points out that although the people of Europe at that time were prepared to believe in mermaids and all kinds of other incredible things, they could not believe in a bird that built its own incubator, so Careri's tale was rejected as just another sailor's yarn.

The early settlers in Australia found large mounds in the scrub well inland and thought that these were big sand castles that the Aboriginal mothers had made to amuse their children. In the north of the continent, later settlers found even bigger mounds and they presumed that these were monuments, or tombs of dead warriors. The Aborigines denied building the mounds either for their children or for their dead but said they were birds' nests. Still nobody believed them. Finally, in 1840, the naturalist John Gilbert decided to test the Aborigines' story in the only reasonable manner possible. He dug into the mounds and there found the eggs.

class	**Aves**
order	**Galliformes**
family	**Megapodidae**
genus & species	***Leipoa ocellata***

△ *Wrapped up in itself: the green mamba, contrary to popular opinion, leads a quiet existence of its own in the trees, and is rarely aggressive.*

Roebild

Mamba

Feared throughout Africa for its deadly venom and remarkable agility, the mamba is one of the most dangerous snakes in the world. The largest is the black or blackmouthed mamba, not in fact black, but dark brown. The usual length is 8 – 9 ft but it may go up to 14 ft. The green mamba never exceeds 9 ft and is usually about 6 ft long. It is shy and elusive, seldom aggressive and its venom is barely half as poisonous as that of the black mamba. The two mambas were once thought to be colour varieties of one species.

The black mamba ranges from the east of Zaire and southern Ethiopia southwards to Natal and South West Africa. One species of green mamba is found on the eastern side of Africa, from Kenya to southern Natal, another two across East Africa and into West Africa. Stories of crested mambas come from older black mambas; their skin is often incompletely moulted and old skin remains attached, especially to the head. The black mamba lives in dry open bush, from lowlands to 4 000 ft, the green mamba lives in trees.

Retreat in anger

Black mambas live on the ground, sometimes wandering far afield, hunting or seeking a mate, but soon returning to a 'home' in a hole in the ground, among rocks or under a fallen tree trunk. The holes are usually aardvark burrows and cavities in termite mounds. If disturbed, they make for home, attacking anything in the way.

Besides the relatively high speed with which it moves the black mamba can strike accurately in any direction, even while travelling fast, with its head raised off the ground, mouth open and tongue flicking. It also expands the neck to form a slight hood and when disturbed gives a hollow-sounding hiss. In striking it can throw its head upwards from the ground for about $\frac{2}{3}$ the length of its body. The speed of mambas is legendary, and has been variously estimated at 10, 20 or 30 mph on the flat and higher estimates have been based on a mamba travelling down a slope. These are completely unrealistic. As a cold-blooded creature with somewhat inefficient circulation, a mamba would not be capable of the effort needed to reach and sustain such speeds. Eyewitness accounts of high speed are sure to be inaccurate; few people would stay and objectively observe a mamba at full speed across rough country. The black mamba is, however, the fastest of snakes,

with an accurately recorded speed of 7 mph. Speeds of about 15 mph may be possible in short bursts. Mambas are at a disadvantage on a smooth surface and black mambas are often run over when crossing roads, especially those with tarred surfaces.

Black mambas will climb into low trees but are more given to climbing rocks, where they lie sunning themselves. The green mamba is a tree-dweller and seldom found outside forests or thick bush. It is slightly less nervous than the black mamba.

The black bird snatcher

The black mamba's prey is almost solely warm-blooded animals, such as birds and small mammals, including dassies or rock hyraxes and rodents. It digests food quickly, a large rat being completely digested in 8 – 10 hours. RM Isemonger, in *Snakes of Africa*, has written about three mambas that basked on a large boulder covered with red-flowered creeper whose blossoms attracted small sugarbirds. As these gathered nectar from the flowers a mamba would suddenly seize one in the air. Within two minutes the bird ceased to struggle and the snake would either swallow it at once or, more often, it would drop the bird on the rock and flicker its tongue over it before eating it. Isemonger also saw a dassie struck as it stopped on the rock to scratch its ear. The dassie ran for cover and after a few minutes the mamba reached into the cover of the vines, seized the corpse, dropped it onto the rock, and, after an inspection with the tongue, swallowed it.

The green mamba eats birds and their eggs, chameleons, geckos and other tree lizards, as well as small mammals.

Rapid growth

Both mambas lay eggs, those of the green mamba being slightly the smaller. The breeding season is spring and early summer. A female black mamba lays 9–14 eggs, oval and 3 in. long. The newly hatched young are 15–24 in. long and able to kill mice or rats. Growth is rapid and one black mamba grew to 6 ft long in a year. A further indication that growth is rapid is that those best acquainted with these reptiles say that a mamba less than 6 ft long is rare. Young black mambas are greyish green to olive green at birth, gradually getting darker as they grow. Baby green mambas are bluish but become brighter green as they grow.

Striking at soft skin

Mambas' main enemies are mongooses, but only while they are young. Eagles and secretary birds kill them and young ones may be eaten by snake-eating snakes. Interesting sidelights are supplied by PW Willis of South Africa on how a mamba kills, and indirectly, on the value of a mongoose's coat as a shield. Willis has had five dogs killed by black mambas and he noticed that in every case the snake struck deliberately and unhurriedly at places where there is soft skin exposed with a minimum of hair, such as behind the ear, on the cheek below the eye or in the 'armpit'. A mongoose, with the exception of the face, lacks these vulnerable spots. Another interesting point in Willis' account is that he said that within a

▽ *World's fastest snake: black mamba at speed.*

A Markowitz

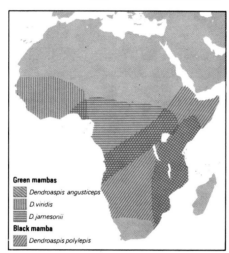

Green mambas
- Dendroaspis angusticeps
- D. viridis
- D. jamesonii

Black mamba
- Dendroaspis polylepis

◁ *Black mamba in right hand, pythons in left. Venom is 'milked' from mambas for research into antidotes and other medical uses.*

few hours each carcase had turned colour and putrefied slightly. This may indicate that the venom is an aid to digestion.

Know your snake!

There are stories about the green mamba lying in wait on branches overhanging paths through the bush, harmonising with the green foliage around it and ready to attack. It is even said to cry out with a weird noise to lure people into its ambush. Then, raising its head and body high, it strikes, sinking its poisonous fangs into the throat of its victim, who drops to the ground paralysed and is dead within seconds. Such stories contrast with what we know of this shy, elusive and unaggressive snake that feeds on lizards and small birds and their eggs. Perhaps it is as well that the green mamba is relatively inoffensive because it is often mistaken for other tree snakes, including harmless species and this misled a student of snakes who parked his car under some trees near Nairobi. On his return he saw a small green snake on top of the car. His thoughts being elsewhere at the moment, he picked up the snake and put it in his pocket. He was horrified to discover later that he had been carrying a green mamba almost next to his skin.

class	**Reptilia**
order	**Squamata**
suborder	**Serpentes**
family	**Elapidae**
genus & species	***Dendroaspis angusticeps*** green mamba ***D. polylepis*** black mamba, others

Nolly Zaloumis

Manakin

Manakins are small titmouse-sized birds that live in the forests of Central and South America and Trinidad. They are stockily built with stout bodies, comparatively large heads and short tails and wings. The males are conspicuous with splashes of colour and sometimes crests or elaborate tails. The females, in contrast, are usually green and very inconspicuous. The yellow-thighed manakin is one of the most conspicuous birds in the forests of Central America, despite its small size. Its plumage is velvety black and the male has a red head and neck. The bill, eyes and the thighs are yellow. The plumage of the male black and white manakin, one of the common forest birds of Trinidad, is black and white with orange legs but the female is olive green with orange legs. The golden-headed manakin is probably even more abundant and certainly more handsome. The male is black with a golden orange cap and red and white thighs. The female is olive green.

Forest birds

Short wings and short tails are typical of small birds—like manakins—that live in forests. They are commonly seen flitting through the foliage in search of fruit and small animals, such as spiders and insects. These are snapped up by the manakins while still in flight and carried back to a perch to be eaten. Fruit makes up the bulk of their diet, however, and manakins have an extremely wide gape that enables them to swallow fruits ¾ in. across. Manakins also join flocks of other small birds in following army ant hordes to catch the small animals which they drive from cover.

Elaborate courtship

Male manakins are so conspicuous because they spend a lot of their time displaying. They display for much of the year, leaving their display grounds only to eat and drink. Each male has a special display ground called a court. Gould's manakin and the black and white manakin clear small patches of ground, about 3 ft by 2 ft, of all leaves, twigs and roots, while the yellow-thighed and golden-headed manakins display from perches on saplings. There may be 50 or more courts in a small area and David Snow, who studied manakins in Trinidad, wrote 'that it is difficult to describe the activities in terms suitable for a scientific paper and at the same time give an adequate impression of the bizarre postures and movements . . . and the extraordinary vivacity of the whole performance'.

Studying the displays is very difficult because it is hard to see the extremely rapid movements of the manakins amongst the foliage. Most of the displays, which are very stereotyped, consist of leaping about the court from perch to perch. The black and white manakin jumps from perch to perch turning around in the air so it is facing the way it came and is ready to jump again. Each

Constance P Warner

jump takes a fraction of a second and it is very difficult to see what is happening. The displays are enhanced by songs and wing noises. The primary flight feathers are narrow and stiff and produce a whirring noise in flight. The shafts of the secondaries are very stout and the vanes stiff and produce a loud snap during some displays.

Female manakins are attracted to the courting males. As a female arrives, the displays become more intense until she becomes attracted to one male. The males of the blue-backed manakin dance in pairs. When a female arrives they circle like a 'big-wheel' at a fair. One flies up and backwards while the other lands in its place. Then the second flies up as the first lands again. After mating with one of them, she flies away and rears the brood by herself.

Growing up without father

The female manakin makes a small nest 1–10 ft up in the fork of a branch. It is made of dead leaves, rootlets and fungi bound together with cobwebs. The female lays 2 eggs and sits on, rather than in, the

◁ *Long-tailed manakin takes a break from the display floor where it spends much of its time.*

nest to incubate them. At first she is easily disturbed but as incubation proceeds she gets bolder and it is sometimes possible to stroke a female as she sits. Alexander Skutch, an authority on tropical American birds, once tried to lift a manakin off to examine the eggs, but she clung to the nest with her feet.

Incubation takes 18–19 days. The chicks are naked and their eyes do not open for 5 days. Their mother feeds them on insects and fruit. The diet contains a large proportion of insects, as is usual in fruit-eating birds whose chicks need extra protein for growth. The chicks stay in the nest for a fortnight then rest hidden in the foliage until they can follow their mother.

Emancipated males

When the males of a species of bird are brightly coloured and the females drab, it is very likely that the males have little to do with caring for the young. The males' colours are an advantage in attracting a female but a decided disadvantage in keeping the nest hidden from predators. Once the male has given up parental duties he can be freed from a permanent link with the female and can develop elaborate plumage and displays. This can only happen in fruit- and nectar-eating species when the female can easily find enough food to feed the chicks herself. In manakins and other forest birds the clutch size is small which also reduces the labour involved in feeding the offspring. To be an advantage, the communal displaying by several males must be more attractive to females than solitary displaying. Because the males stimulate each other to greater activity their communal 'attraction' is greater than the sum of the 'attraction' of the same number of solitary males. The intense attraction also rapidly reduces the shyness of the female. In normal pair formation it takes some time for the female to accept the male, and often for the male not to behave aggressively towards her, but in a promiscuous society as in manakins and others such as capercaillie (p. 499) it is essential for the female to be able to mate with a male with few preliminaries.

The female's ability to choose her mate out of several suitors has led to the evolution of elaborate displays including the mechanical sounds and plumage to impress her. It has been found that some male manakins attract more females than others but the basis of their attraction is unknown.

class	**Aves**
order	**Passeriformes**
family	**Pipridae**
genera & species	***Chiroxiphia pareola*** *blue-backed manakin*
	Manacus manacus *black and white manakin*
	M. vitellinus *Gould's manakin*
	Pipra erythrocephala *golden-headed manakin*
	P. mentalis *yellow-thighed manakin*

Manatee

With split lips and hairy, creased faces, the sea cows known as manatees make grotesquely inadequate mermaids—yet some people ascribe the legend to them. There are 3 species, one along the coast and in certain large rivers of West Africa, one in the Caribbean from the southeastern United States to northern South America and one in the estuaries of the Orinoco and the Amazon. Like the related dugong (p. 808) they are fish-shaped, up to 15 ft long and 1 500 lb weight, with hairless skin, paddle-like forelimbs and horizontal tail which is broadly rounded and shovel-like, not divided into two lobes as in the dugong. The flippers are mobile and can be used as hands. The colour is dark grey to blackish. There are further differences in the face; there are no front teeth and the bristly upper lip is divided and mobile, the two opposing halves being used as a grasping organ for plucking underwater vegetation. Manatees have 6 neck vertebrae instead of the usual 7.

A life of ease

Manatees must rank among the world's most inoffensive large mammals. Singly, or in groups of 15—20, they swim sluggishly and deliberately in sea, coastal lagoons and rivers. Inquisitive creatures, they will investigate any strange objects, like fishing boats, coming close and peering at them myopically—their eyesight is not good. When not feeding they rest at the surface with only the arched back exposed or, in shallow waters, they may 'stand' with the tail bent under the hind end of the body, and with the head and shoulders out of water. In shallow water they will sometimes walk on the tips of the flippers. Adults swim with the tail, using the flippers to turn, but the babies swim with flippers. They usually surface every 5—10 minutes to take 2—3 breaths, but they can remain underwater for 16 minutes so long as they are inactive.

Living weed-killer

Manatees are active at any hour but feed mainly at night on aquatic plants, especially eelgrass and they will pluck leaves from land plants overhanging water. The forceps-like lips grip food, and the bristles help push it in perhaps with some help from the paddles.

They seem to eat any vegetation within reach, provided it is not too tough to be pulled apart with the lips.

Manatees' large appetites and their readiness to take any vegetation growing in water suggested they might be used to clear ponds or rivers of weed. Since 1885 they have kept free the ornamental pools in the Botanic Gardens in Georgetown, and in 1960 there was hope that manatees might be used to clear the water hyacinth that was spreading in the tropics of Africa and America, choking waterways. Only limited success was obtained because manatees did not tolerate being transported or corralled and generally kept in semi-domestication.

Brief, playful courtship

When we consider that manatees have attracted a fair share of attention for at least 500 years, it is surprising how little we know of their way of life. For example, they seem to have a courtship. There is no distinct breeding season. The female in oestrus is followed by males for 2—4 weeks, although she is receptive only briefly. Copulation is horizontal, in water over 6 ft deep. The female is promiscuous when in heat. A dozen manatees come together and move as a herd into shallow water. There they pair

Manatee
- Amazon & Orinoco *(Trichechus inunguis)*
- Caribbean *(T. manatus)*
- West African *(T. senegalensis)*

off, making a great commotion in the water. The pairs then drag themselves half out of the water and embrace lying on their sides. After this they return to the water and play vigorously as a herd. The whole courtship, mating and the play that follows it take 10–15 minutes after which the manatees go their separate ways.

There is usually only one calf at a birth, occasionally two, born under water and immediately brought to the surface by the mother to take the first breath. The gestation period is 152–180 days. The baby is pink, 3 ft long and weighs up to 60 lb. It becomes mature at 2–3 years old, when about 8 ft long. Manatees in zoos have not survived for long, but it is thought they may live for more than 50 years.

There is a difference of opinion on the part of observers about how the mother suckles her baby. The teats are near the 'armpits' and some say the mother lies belly up, others that she lies belly down, with the calf at her side. Sometimes it seems she will clasp the baby to her with a flipper while she is vertical with her head and shoulders out of water, in a somewhat human fashion. Charnock-Wilson, after questioning people in British Honduras, believes this is exceptional behaviour for manatees.

◁ *Visitors feed manatees at the Botanic Gardens, Georgetown, Guyana.*
▷ *Manatees seem to eat any vegetation within reach, provided it is not too tough to be pulled apart with the two lobes of the powerful, prehensile upper lip.*
▽ *It is remarkable that these strange-looking creatures should have been confused with the sirens of ancient mythology but this is how their family name was derived. It is said that they reminded sailors of mermaids because they nurse their young like humans.*
▷▽ *These fish-shaped mammals can be up to 15 ft long and 1 500 lb. in weight. All photos show Caribbean manatee* **Trichechus manatus.**

Sacrificed to sport

Manatees have few enemies other than alligators and man. They have been killed for their flesh and hides by the local peoples for centuries but in the last decade or so have been protected by law in several places in tropical America. Perhaps the biggest menace today is the disturbance of their habitat by the increasing use of outboard motorboats, especially for sport.

Horrible sea-food?

It is sometimes said that manatees gave rise to the stories of mermaids. The only basis for this is that Christopher Columbus noted in his journal, for January 1493, that when off the coast of Haiti he saw three mermaids that rose well out of the water. His opinion of them was that they were not as beautiful as they had been painted although to some extent they were like a man in face. Later Columbus realized they were manatees, which he had probably met before on the coast of West Africa. During the 16th century Konrad von Gessner, the Swiss naturalist, and William Rondelet, a physician of Montpellier, both of whom wrote massive books on natural history, included the manatee as a fish although even then it was called *Vacca marina* or sea-cow. Ulysses Aldrovandus, professor of medicine and philosophy at Bologna, also included the manatee in his large treatise on fishes, published in 1613. John Ray, the Father of English Natural History, writing in 1693, guided solely by the fact that the manatee was said to have a body like man, thought it was a biped but included it among the quadrupeds. The people who ran the plantations in the West Indies were less concerned with its place in the animal kingdom. They used its meat to feed their slaves. Emil Hanson, collector for the Miami Seaquarium, is reported to have said that he is not aware of another sea creature tasting more horrible.

class	**Mammalia**
order	**Sirenia**
family	**Trichechidae**
genus & species	*Trichechus inunguis* Amazon and Orinoco **T. manatus** Caribbean **T. senegalensis** West Africa

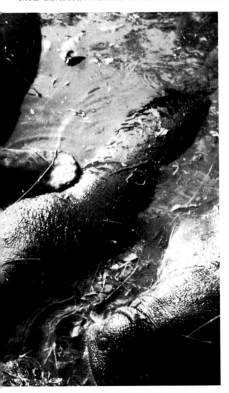

Photos by Popperfoto

Mandrill

Nobody who has been to a zoo where the mandrill is kept can have failed to have noticed it or to have been impressed by its colourful, even repulsive appearance.

The mandrill is a forest-living baboon and, with its close relative the drill, differs so strongly in some respects from other baboons that the two are singled out here for special attention.

The mandrill's body is thick-set, up to 33 in. long, with a stumpy tail only 4 in. long. The muzzle is long and deep and has long thick ridges on either side of the nose. The nostrils are broad and round and the male has long sabre-like canine teeth. The male mandrill is brightly coloured and most people who have seen it remember the colours on its face and the colours it presents as it turns and walks away. The general colour of its coat is dark brown with white cheek whiskers, yellow beard and a crest on the crown of the head. The nose is bright red and the ridges on the muzzle are an equally bright blue. His genitalia have a similar colouring and there is also a blue patch on the rump, on either side of the ischial callosities, or sitting-pads, which are pink. The female is altogether more drab; her face is grey black and her genitalia are not brightly coloured.

The drill is slightly smaller than the mandrill, being up to 28 in. long and its general colour is olive-brown, the face is a deep black and there are no grooves on the muzzle ridges. The drill has, however, a white fringe round the face.

The mandrill is restricted to Cameroun, Rio Muni, Gabon and Zaire. The drill is found in Gabon and Cameroun, to the Cross River in Nigeria, also on Fernando Póo, but strangely it does not occur in Rio Muni. Both live in tropical rain forest, the drill to quite high altitudes on Mount Cameroun.

Okapia

△ *Mandrill manners: a yawn means aggression rather than tiredness in primate language.*
▽ *Like father, like son: a zoo-bred youngster.*

▷ *Mandrill magnificence: the exposed parts of the mandrill's skin, face and hindquarters, are the most highly coloured of any mammal.*

Secret vegetarians

Mandrills and drills are said to live in small family groups in the wild, with one male and one or more females with their offspring making up each group. They walk on their toes and fingers, the soles and the palms not touching the ground. Although they seem to spend most of their time on the forest floor they climb to the middle layer of the trees to feed and to sleep. Their food in the wild is a matter for speculation. Probably, like other baboons living on the savannah, they eat mainly plant food together with a certain amount of insects and other animal food. It is likely, however, that their diet is more vegetarian than that of other baboons.

Monthly breeding cycle

In 1937 a baby mandrill was born at the Chester Zoo, and one was born at the London Zoo in 1953. In the United States,

Beringero Pampaluchi: Bavaria

The drill's face is deep black, opposite to the mandrill's colourful visage and also lacks the grooves on the muzzle ridges.

however, births in zoos have been more common. Mandrills usually bear one baby at a time, but twins were born in the Zoological Gardens of Baltimore in 1961. The female is in season every 33 days and this is shown externally by the swelling around her genitalia, which begins after menstruation and reaches a peak at ovulation. There seems to be no special season for breeding. The development of the young is similar to that of other baboons (p. 268) and in monkeys generally. In zoos mandrills are long-lived; one reached $26\frac{1}{2}$ years and another 46.

Why the colours?

Mandrills and drills are among the largest of the baboons and they are the most fearsome to look at, as well as being the most powerful. Leopards may take the babies from time to time but they certainly would not attack a full-grown male. The fearsome appearance is to some extent due to the colours, and zoologists, especially those who study animal behaviour, have been hard put to it to suggest what purpose the colouring serves. Wolfgang Wickler has suggested that the mandrill being highly coloured at both

ends tends to baffle his enemies. He puts it this way, that a flash of colour from the mandrill's rear end would make a potential enemy quake and run away, thinking that what was in fact a mandrill going away from him was a mandrill coming towards him. Few zoologists feel tempted to accept this theory, at least in its present form. Ramona and Desmond Morris, in their book *Men and Apes*, have offered an alternative theory, which is perhaps slightly more plausible. We know that in some monkeys, such as the vervets, the males have brightly coloured genitalia and two males will show these colours to each other as a form of threat display. The Morris's theory is that the mandrill uses its colours in much the same way, but having a coloured face as well there is a double impact of threat towards an opponent. One drawback to this theory is that the drill, so closely related to the mandrill and so like it in almost every other way, has only a black face.

The problem of the use of colours by the mandrill is one that probably can be solved only by close study in the wild, and that seems to be a long way off.

Gessner's ape-wolf

The Swiss naturalist Konrad von Gessner, who lived in the 16th century, has left us valuable records of the contemporary knowledge of natural history, some based on travellers' tales, others on fact. One such tale concerned an animal that he called an ape-wolf or bear-wolf. Gessner wrote: 'This animal was brought to Augsburg with great wonder and was shown in the year 1551. It is found in the great wilderness of the Indian land but is very rare. On its feet it has fingers like a man, and when anyone points at it, it turns its buttocks to him. It is by nature frolicsome especially towards women, to whom it displays its frolicsomeness.' It is now believed that Gessner's ape-wolf was the mandrill.

class	**Mammalia**
order	**Primates**
family	**Cercopithecidae**
genus & species	***Papio sphinx*** *mandrill* ***P. leucophaeus*** *drill*

Maneater shark

A single species of heavy-bodied shark bears the ominous name of maneater, or great white shark. It grows to a length of 36½ ft and is bluish-grey to slate grey above, shading to white below, with fins growing darker towards their edges. It also has a conspicuous black spot just behind where the pectoral fin joins the body. Its snout is pointed and overhangs an awesome, crescent-shaped mouth which is armed with a frightful array of triangular saw-edged teeth. In large individuals the largest teeth may be 3 in. high. The pectoral fins are large. The pelvic fins, and the second dorsal and the anal fins, which lie opposite each other, are small. The tail fin is nearly symmetrical instead of having the upper lobe larger as in most sharks. There is a large keel along the side of the tail in front of the tail fin.

The maneater belongs to the family of mackerel sharks, which includes the porbeagles and mako shark. These are similar to the maneater but smaller, up to 12 ft long being about the limit. They feed on

young alive. The maneater is said to be of uncertain temper, yet skin divers report it to be wary and even easily scared. It is probably less dangerous than the mako which is known to attack small boats as well as swimmers. The maneater's bad reputation probably rests on its large size and fearsome teeth, coupled with occasional attacks that look deliberate. On the first of these two points it is hard to speak with certainty. The largest maneater of which we have reliable information measured 36½ ft long, and this one was caught a century ago, off Port Fairey, Australia. Most of the others are between 20 and 25 ft. One that was 21 ft long weighed 7 100 lb; another 17 ft long weighed 2 800 lb. Maneaters have been said by authoritative writers to grow to over 40 ft but there is no solid evidence.

Nothing refused
Several books have been published in the last 20 years which give details of shark attacks. Two are devoted solely to the subject. They are: *Shark Attack* by VM Coppleson, an Australian doctor who has collected the case histories of injuries from sharks, and *Danger Shark!* by Jean Campbell Butler, whose narrative is based on the New Orleans Shark Conference of 1958, at which shark researchers pooled their findings. Putting the information from these and other

swallowed take days, even weeks, to be digested. The other, which seems linked with this but is learned more from sharks in captivity, is that sharks seem to eat little.

Extenuating circumstances
When one speaks of malice in relation to shark attack one is only reflecting the attitude of mariners to these beasts. As a class they are hated. There are many stories of captured sharks being treated with savagery, being disembowelled and then thrown back live into the sea. Yet in the economy of the sea they are scavengers rather than evil predators. Moreover, in areas where shark attack is heavy there is reason to suppose man has not been blameless. For example, in the region around Sydney Harbour, Australia, and again at Florida, blood from abattoirs seeps into the sea, and sharks are drawn by the smell of blood. In the Bay of Bengal, where human corpses are floated down the Ganges from the burning ghats, shark attack is again high.

None of these things lessens one's sympathy for victims of shark attack, nor lessens one's own fear of the sharks themselves, but they put the subject in perspective zoologically. One of the first scientific conclusions we are led to is that while sharks may be ferocious they seem not to be voracious, as they are so often described. In fact,

A Sycholt: Bavaria

Maligned monster: the maneater shark's bad reputation stems from its large size and supposed voraciousness. Most maneaters measure between 20 and 25 ft and not 40 ft as often quoted. They seem to eat anything that looks like food which results in bathers, corpses, carrion and rubbish being taken.

fishes such as mackerel, herring, cod, whiting, hake and dogfish. They also provide sport for sea anglers because of the fight they put up when hooked. Most mackerel sharks are dangerous to man.

The maneater is found in all warm seas and occasionally strays into temperate seas. It lives in the open sea, coming inshore only when the shallow seas are near deep water. One maneater was caught at a depth of 4 200 ft off Cuba and other evidence also suggests the shark is a deepwater fish.

Not as big as was believed
Maneaters may be much maligned monsters. They are neither as big as is generally said nor as voracious. Very little is known about the habits of the maneater except what can be deduced from its shape and the contents of the stomachs of individuals caught and dissected. Its shape suggests it can swim rapidly, but from those hooked and landed with angling tackle it is fairly certain the maneater is not as swift as the smaller mako. Since young have been found in a female's body the species is presumed to bear its

sources together, there is the general impression that sharks, the maneater in particular, will try to eat anything that looks like food. As a result they snap at living animals, including bathers or people who have accidentally fallen into the sea, as well as corpses and carrion, even inanimate objects such as tin cans. The attacks on boats, as in the attack on the 14ft cod boat off Nova Scotia in 1953, by a maneater, which left some of its teeth in the timbers, are probably due to mistake rather than malice. Several times whole human corpses have been taken from sharks' stomachs but they proved to be of people who had been drowned.

Maneater or corpse swallower?
There are several instances of maneaters found to contain the intact bodies of other animals. These include a 100lb sea-lion, a 50lb seal, and sharks 6–7 ft long. While human beings have been badly bitten, usually producing frightful wounds, some of which have proved fatal, there is little evidence of limbs being severed, and less of a person being swallowed whole. Two things have also emerged from the studies so far made. The first is that sharks digest food very slowly and animal remains

because they will engulf almost anything they come across, sharks have at times aided the course of human justice.

Silent witness

The classic example of this concerned the United States brig *Nancy* which was captured on July 3, 1799 by HM Cutter *Sparrow* and taken to Port Royal, Jamaica, Britain and the United States then being at war, to be condemned as a prize. The captain of the *Nancy* produced papers at the trial which were, in fact, false and he was about to be discharged when another British warship put in at the port with papers found in a shark caught on August 30. They proved to be the ship's papers thrown overboard by the captain of the *Nancy,* when capture seemed inevitable. They led to the condemnation of the brig and her cargo.

class	**Chondrichthyes**
order	**Lamniformes**
family	**Charcharodontidae**
genus & species	***Carcharodon carcharias***

◁ *Giant fox on stilts: the most striking of the dog family comes from southern Brazil, Paraguay and the north of Argentina, in regions where small areas of forest are interspersed with more open country. It is seldom seen because it is solitary and secretive, usually hunting at night for insects, birds and mammals.*
▽ *Triplets 25 days old.* ▽▽ *Twins 45 days old.*

Mock battles between 5-month-old maned wolves. Their behaviour in the wild has not been studied, but the dog family behave in much the same way. The movements of the tail, ear and mouth plus the overall body posture are the main components of their language.
◁ *Threat.* ▽ *Attack.* ◁▽ *Defeat.*

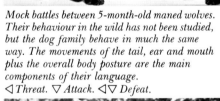

Klages : Bavaria

Okapia

Okapia

Okapia

Okapia

Okapia

Maned wolf

The maned wolf is a South American fox. It looks like a large red fox on stilts because of its long legs. Head and body together measure 51 in., and the tail 16 in. It stands 2½ ft at the shoulder and weighs up to 51 lb. Apart from the northern wolf it is the largest member of the dog family. Its coat is shaggy and yellowish red and the legs are black for most of their length. There is some black about the mouth, and sometimes on the back and tail. The tip of the tail, chin and throat are sometimes white. Its name is from a mane on the back of the neck and shoulders which is erected in moments of excitement.

It ranges from the southern parts of Brazil to the Argentine.

Long legs puzzle

The maned wolf is solitary, mainly nocturnal and speedy. Like other foxes, it is shy and wary of man. Not surprisingly, therefore, little is known of its habits. It lives where small areas of forest are interspersed with open country, and it can be assumed that in foraging it ranges widely over the countryside. Otherwise its extraordinarily long legs have no meaning unless they are an adaptation for seeing above the long grass while running through it. This seems unlikely since the maned wolf lives on small prey that could not be seen any the better from a height of 2 ft. It is said that maned wolves are agile when going uphill but clumsy when descending, because their hindlegs are slightly longer than their forelegs.

Banana addict

The prey is said to be pacas and agoutis, both of them large and fast-running rodents, also insects, reptiles and birds. The maned wolf eats fruit, sugar cane and other plant foods. In fact, maned wolves have been successfully kept alive in the Antwerp Zoo on 2 pigeons and 4½ lb of bananas a day. Other foods were tried but lean meat was brought up, and eggs and milk were refused. Three maned wolves in the San Diego Zoo took only bananas at first but later turned from these and were fed cubed meat. In the wild, the wolves dig out snails from soft ground and also small rodents. Surprisingly they dig with their teeth, and are said never to use the claws for digging, which if true must be unique for a carnivore.

Pups like fox cubs

Courtship is similar to that of domestic dogs. The number of pups is usually two but there were three litters of three each born in the San Diego Zoo in 1953-4. The baby coats are dark brown, nearly black, and the tails have white tips. Unfortunately none of these survived so nothing is known of the later growth stages. The record life span in captivity is 10½ years.

Fastest dog

There are no natural enemies, yet there is a real fear that maned wolves may soon become extinct. Having no thick underfur, their pelts are useless. The animals themselves are not common in zoos. The reason why they are becoming rare is that they are killed because of alleged attacks on lambs, calves and foals. One way they are hunted is on horseback, with a lasso. The wolf is vulnerable to this because, having no enemies, it merely runs for a while then stops and looks round. The idea of continuous flight seems to be absent from its makeup, so it fails to make the most use of its speed, which is said to be greater than that of any other member of the dog family, and comparable with that of the cheetah in the cat family.

Unusually sweet-toothed

In many ways the so-called South American foxes are fox-like, yet they resemble dogs in other ways. Their English common names reflect this. Besides the maned wolf and the bushdog there are the crab-eating fox, the small-eared dog and others, of which Azara's dog is one. It looks like a short-legged fox but in its anatomy is much nearer the wolf and the jackal. Its home is in the forests of Paraguay and northern Argentina where it feeds much as the maned wolf does, on insects, lizards, small mammals and ground birds. Like the maned wolf it eats seeds and fruits. It has also developed a liking for sugar cane and will leave the shelter of its forest home to create havoc among the cane crop. More than this, it seems to have an obsession for the sweet sap and will slash and chew the canes as if its life depended on it.

class	**Mammalia**	
order	**Carnivora**	
family	**Canidae**	
genera & species	***Chrysocyon brachyurus*** *maned wolf* ***Dusicyon azarae*** *Azara's dog*	

With pointed muzzle, very large erect ears and body covered with long, reddish-brown hair the handsome maned wolf reclines peacefully.

roebild

Mangabey

Mangabeys are large long-tailed monkeys, bigger and stronger than most monkeys. They live in trees and have, in the past, been thought of as typical monkeys, like guenons and macaques. The modern view is that they are essentially tree-living baboons closely related to the mandrill. They have rather long black faces with deep hollows under the cheek bones and white upper eyelids. As in baboons the skin around the female's genitalia swells up each month as she comes into season and the males have large ischial callosities, or sitting-pads. These features plus their larger size make mangabeys more like the baboons than any other monkeys.

The various species can be separated into two groups. In the first group, which includes the collared, sooty and gold-bellied mangabeys, the hair is short and speckled, the lower parts of the limbs are darker than the body and the underparts are white or yellow. They have no crest on the head, the eyelids are startlingly white and the tail is slightly longer than head and body combined. The second group, which includes the grey-cheeked and black mangabeys have a long black coat which is grey on the underparts. They often have ear tufts and always have a tuft on the head. In the black mangabey this stands up in a point and in the grey-cheeked falls untidily in all directions. The tail in this group is half as long again as head and body combined. All mangabeys are 18–24 in. long, the females being smaller than the males.

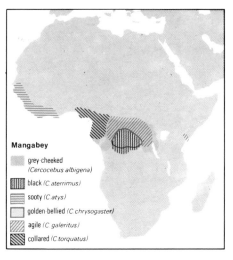

Mangabey

grey-cheeked
(Cercocebus albigena)

black (C. aterrimus)

sooty (C. atys)

golden-bellied (C. chrysogaster)

agile (C. galeritus)

collared (C. torquatus)

The first group, the mangabeys lacking a crest, live in the forests from Senegal east to the gallery forest at the mouth of the Tana River. These live on the ground and in the trees in all kinds of forest. The second group, the crested mangabeys, are restricted to the tall dense forests of Zaire.

Tell-tale tails

Mangabeys sit and carry their tails in an often characteristic fashion. The grey-cheeked and black hold their tails straight up with the tip usually arched forward above the back, when they are standing still or walking slowly. The collared and sooty mangabeys hold their tails out behind, slightly bowed and curled at the tip when they are running along a branch and when standing still the tail tends to be arched right over the back with the tip hanging down over the head. When sitting on a branch, collared mangabeys support themselves on their hands and feet like most mammals but the grey-cheeked rest on their rumps with their feet and hands together in front of them and their legs and arms akimbo on either side.

Three meals a day

Mangabeys feed mainly on fruit; crestless mangabeys raid crops as well. Their day starts soon after dawn around 6.30–7.10. At first they merely move around rather aimlessly as we tend to do first thing in the morning. They take their first meal of the day between 8 and 9 am and then they rest. They take another meal about mid-day, have another rest and take their third meal between 4 and 5 pm. The scientific way of expressing this is that they have three feeding peaks during the day. Guenons, who often feed with the mangabeys, have only two peaks and this prevents the two kinds of monkeys getting in each other's way at feeding times.

The females groom the males a great deal especially during the afternoon when the troop is resting. As with baboons the males rarely or never groom the females.

Unsociable males

Mangabeys breed at all times of the year. The female has a monthly sexual cycle, as in the baboons. Almost hairless at birth, the baby mangabeys cling to their mother's belly fur for transport. Some of the adult males will show a fair amount of interest in the infants, sometimes carrying them around and cuddling them. Once independent of their parents they tend to associate in groups and avoid the adults. It is not possible to say more about the social behaviour of mangabeys with any degree of confidence because apparently it can vary from species to species as well as from place to place. For example, in Rio Muni, grey-cheeked mangabeys live in groups of 9–11 with only

◁ Banana breakfast for collared mangabey. ▽ Concentrating deeply on her cleaning task, a collared mangabey mother grooms a juvenile.

Young grey-cheeked mangabey will on maturity have head crest and long black coat as seen in adult above.

Uni-sex eye makeup: with raised eyebrows exposing prominent almost white upper lids collared mangabeys show threat.

one adult male in each group. The same species in Uganda lives in groups of 15–20 with 4 or 5 adult males in each group, which is much the same as in the collared mangabey. Where there is more than one male in a group they tend to avoid each other and may wander off on their own for a while.

Several ways of meeting danger

Probably the main enemy of all forest monkeys in Africa is the crowned eagle, and this is true for mangabeys. Leopards and pythons no doubt take their toll as well, and man has played his part. The behaviour of the different species in moments of danger varies a good deal. Collared mangabeys will stop calling and stay very quiet but grey-cheeked mangabeys call all the more. When further threatened the grey-cheeked will rapidly escape into the tallest trees but the collared runs across the top of the tree canopy, where it is continuous, or goes down to the ground, in both cases moving into swamp forest for protection. They use their exceptional leaping ability – they can jump as much as 20 ft – when moving around on branches but by comparison with some other monkeys, for example, the guenons, their movements appear slow and deliberate.

White-black mangabey

From time to time somebody sees a pure white starling in a flock and gets quite excited about it. Or it may be a pure white sparrow or an albino squirrel. Undoubtedly people are interested in these freaks. The question of how rare these albinos are often arises. It is virtually impossible to answer such a question because no census has ever been taken of any one population over a period of years in order to assess it. Albinism varies from one species to another. And here we come to a rather striking fact. The black mangabey, although so well known by name, is rarely seen in zoos and of the comparatively small numbers of known individuals of this species almost one third have been albinos. It is ironic that this should happen in the black mangabey. It may, however, be no more than a coincidence. If we look through the books on British mammals written up to about 1950 we shall, as likely as not, read that albino moles, for example, are common, yet mole catchers who have spent a lifetime trapping moles and have had 10 000 or so pass through their hands have never seen one.

In the Mammal Section in the Natural History Museum in London there are (or

were) two drawers containing the skins of the common mole. The skins in one drawer were all from albino moles, the skins in the other drawer were all from moles of normal colour. To judge from the proportions of these study specimens 50% of moles are white. The truth is that whenever a person found a white mole in past years it was sent to the Museum as a curiosity, whereas nobody bothered to send the skins of moles that were coloured in a normal way. It may well be the same with the black mangabey. When somebody who is collecting for museums sees a white individual he does all he can to capture it because he knows people will be interested in it.

class	**Mammalia**
order	**Primates**
family	**Cercopithecidae**
genus & species	***Cercocebus albigena*** *grey-cheeked mangabey* **C. aterrimus** *black mangabey* **C. atys** *sooty mangabey* **C. chrysogaster** *golden-bellied mangabey* **C. galeritus** *agile mangabey* **C. torquatus** *collared mangabey*

KB Newman

Bronzewing mannikin — tame and cheerful bird with a call like a wheezy twitter. It is common on cultivated land, open country and bush in Africa. These mannikins often roost communally in large untidy grass nests built one on top of the other in bushes or forks of branches.

Mannikin

Mannikins are a group of small seed-eating birds, of which the Java sparrow (p. 1321) is the largest. They are 4–4½ in. long, somewhat smaller than a house sparrow, and sometimes brightly but not gaudily coloured with patches of brown, black and white. The cut-throat and red-headed finch have red on their heads. Two very common species, which are popular as cage birds, are the spice finch and the 'Bengalese finch'. The spice finch, also known as the nutmeg finch, spice bird and spotted or common munia, has a chestnut-brown back with white streaks. The head is reddish-brown, the tail greyish-yellow and the underparts white with faint brown markings. The 'Bengalese finch' is a domestic variety of one subspecies of the striated finch. It has been bred to pro-

duce several colour variations and is unknown in the wild. The chestnut-breasted finch, barley bird or chestnut-breasted munia has a greyish-brown head, with black on the cheeks and throat, a dark brown back, yellow and brown tail, chestnut breast and white underparts. Other mannikins include the magpie mannikin, the bronzewing mannikin and two species of silverbill.

Mannikins are found mainly in the tropics of Asia, ranging from India to New Guinea. Some are found in northern Australia and Africa, and the bib finch lives in Madagascar.

The typical habitat of mannikins is open country, especially near open water. The chestnut-breasted finch of Australia which lives in reeds and grasses alongside marshes and streams, has been encouraged in its spread by increased artificial irrigation.

Three-call language

Mannikins are small, colourful, sociable birds, living in flocks and eating, sleeping and preening together. The spice finch has three calls, each used for a different purpose by members of a flock. As they fly about they utter a quiet 'chip' to keep in touch with each other. A louder 'kit-tee' is used for identification and is heard as the birds go to roost. There is also a sharp creaking alarm call.

Eating dried meat

Mannikins live in open country because they are basically seed-eaters, feeding mainly on the seeds of grasses. They have several different methods of feeding. The spice finch, for example, hops about on the ground feeding on fallen seeds, it climbs tall grasses drawing them together to get at the seed heads and it hangs from vertical twigs to eat seeds on grass heads below. Along with other mannikins, the spice finch is often a pest in fields of rice and other crops. They strip the plants of seeds and also break them under their weight. The spice finch also feeds on refuse such as breadcrumbs and has formed the habit of feeding on the squashed remains of toads and other animals that have been run over. It apparently eats the meat only after it has dried. The chestnut-breasted finch never feeds on the ground like the spice finch, but catches flying termites on the wing, especially during the breeding season, to provide protein for its growing chicks.

Strong nests

The first stage in courtship is for the two mannikins to pick up a blade of grass apiece and fly or hop about excitedly with the grass in their bills. The courtship dance of the spice finch is performed with the male alighting by the female and bowing to her after they have dropped their pieces of grass. He sings a feeble twittering jingle, with tail bent down and feathers fluffed. He also sways from side to side and bobs up and down. The chestnut-breasted finch has a similar courtship but both birds dance, repeatedly bowing to each other, then stretching upwards. The nest is built in trees, or sometimes on buildings, and several may be placed close together to form a colony. It is globular, about 8 in. long, 6 in. in section, with a chamber inside connected to a short entrance tunnel covered by a porch. The materials are grasses and bark, with a lining of soft grasses, and as the materials are laid in orderly layers the walls are strong and very waterproof. The spice finches also build roosting nests where a crowd of them gather for the night.

The eggs, 3–7 in number, are incubated by both parents for about 3 weeks. The chicks grow rapidly and are fully mature in a few months.

Australian invader

The spice finch is a native of Asia, from India and Ceylon to Formosa and the Tanimbar Islands of Indonesia. The Tanimbar Islands are also 200 miles from the coast of Australia but the spice finch never colonised Australia until it escaped from aviaries. It has also been introduced to Hawaii, Mauritius and the Seychelles. The spice finch was first found as a free-living bird in Australia about 1940, around Brisbane. Then it appeared in Sydney and Townsville in 1950. From Townsville it spread northward along the coast of Queensland to Innisfail and Cairns. Settled areas are preferred and the spice finch has become the equivalent of the house sparrow. It is also displacing the native finches such as the zebra finch. This is probably because it has a wider variety of feeding habits and has larger clutches and a longer breeding season than the native finches. The nest of the spice finch is also more strongly built than those of other Australian finches and fewer broods are lost during storms.

Spice or nutmeg finch — prettily mottled mannikin favoured as a cage bird as it is easily bred.

R Longo

class	**Aves**
order	**Passeriformes**
family	**Estrildidae**
genera & species	***Amadina erythrocephala*** redheaded finch
	A. fasciata cut-throat
	Lonchura castaneothorax chestnut-breasted finch
	L. cucullata bronzewing mannikin
	L. fringilloides magpie mannikin
	L. malabarica common silverwing
	L. nana bibfinch
	L. punctulata spice finch
	L. striata striated finch others